Stoicism and Christianity

by Keith Humphrey

Unless otherwise noted, quotes are taken from the following translations:

The New Testament, King James Bible. 1769.

Seneca, Letters on Ethics. Translated by Margaret Graver and A.A.Long, 2015, University of Chicago.

Musonius Rufus, That One Should Disdain Hardships. Translated by Cora E. Lutz, 2020 Yale University.

Epictetus, The Complete Works. Edited and Translated by Robin Waterfield, 2022, University of Chicago.

Marcus Aurelius, The Emperor's Handbook. Translation of the Meditations by C. Scot Hicks and David V. Hicks. 2002, Simon & Schuster.

Introduction

Christians are well-versed in the ways in which Christianity supplanted Judaism. They seem to be less aware of how Christianity supplanted the entire Greco-Roman worldview, including the reigning philosophy of the day, which was Stoicism. Yet this is much more significant in the history of Western Civilization, and a contest that continues to this day; as traditional Christianity wanes in the West, and Stoicism experiences a resurgence.

Christian ideas came face-to-face with the epicenter of Greek Philosophy on Mars Hill; where despite artfully framing his message in the context of their worldview, Paul was laughed off the porch for preaching the resurrection of the dead, which to the Greeks was utter foolishness. Dionysius the Areopagite heard the Apostle and crossed over to become a Christian, however; and this prefigured how Christianity would gain a small foothold which would ultimately prevail, as and Christianity would eventually become the reigning worldview in Greece.

Christianity was largely a matter of indifference to the Stoics, as they did not take it seriously. Paul was brought before the judgment seat of Gallio, the brother of Seneca the Younger, but the case against him was dismissed as irrelevant. Lucius Annaeus Seneca was a tutor to a young Nero, who later rejected a temperate life, and became an avid persecutor of Christians, and even ordered the death of Seneca himself. Around this time, Gaius Musonius Rufus taught Stoicism in Rome, and Epictetus heard him there. Later, Epictetus went on to become perhaps the most influential Stoic teacher of all time. Marcus Aurelius read the works of Epictetus, and journaled his own Stoic thoughts in the *Meditations*. He was considered the last of the good Roman emperors, and manifested the apex of Stoicism as a legendary philosopher-king.

During the imperial reign of Marcus Aurelius, the contest with Christianity reached a turning point with Justin the Philosopher, who after having learned from Stoicism and other schools of thought, converted to Christianity. Justin taught Christianity in Rome as the one true philosophy, and sealed his testimony with martyrdom. The rest is history, as Stoicism faded, and Christianity eventually prevailed over the entire Western world.

In our modern world, while Christianity continues to reign as the most popular worldview, there is a renewed interest in Stoicism. Perhaps due to some watered-down, shallow, self-centered and effeminate flavors of Christianity currently available for mass consumption; people are looking for something more meaningful, with practical application to daily life, and a purposeful discipline which makes for a better man. Does this reveal a fundamental weakness in Christianity which has finally been exposed to the rigors of philosophical inquiry? Is there yet another chapter to be written in this contest of ideas?

If we turn back the pages to consider the philosophical background to the emergence of Christianity, we see that it answered the same questions as to the meaning and purpose of life, while providing a better hope for the afterlife. By comparing some of the early Stoic and Christian writings, I do not mean to suggest that these ideas were shared between them; but only that they concurrently occupied the same space and time, and addressed the same concerns of how we should live in this world. By better understanding the contextual worldview of the beginnings of Christianity, we can better appreciate the meaning and value that it has for all time.

In his letters to his friend Lucilius, Seneca frequently steals proverbs from the rival philosopher Epicurus, justifying it with, "Whatever is said well by anyone belongs to me." (Seneca, Letters. 16.7) . Ironically, Christianity over time also stole many ideas from Stoicism, and later from Platonism, as it adapted itself to become the prevailing worldview in the West, claiming that these ideas came from God in the first place. The Apostle John supplants the very source of the Stoic cosmos, identifying Jesus Christ with the Logos of God, the rational principle which structures and upholds the universe.

> John 1:1-5
> In the beginning was the Word, and the Word was with God, and the Word was God. 2 The same was in the beginning with God. 3 All things were made by him; and without him was not any thing made that was made. 4 In him was life; and the life was the light of men. 5 And the light shineth in darkness; and the darkness comprehended it not.

> John 1:14
> And the Word was made flesh, and dwelt among us, (and we beheld his glory, the glory as of the only begotten of the Father,) full of grace and truth.

Throughout Christian history, Stoic philosophers were often appropriated by Christian theologians.

> Tertullian, A Treatise on the Soul. 20.1,
> https://www.newadvent.org/fathers/0310.htm
> Just as Seneca says, whom we so often find on our side: 'There are implanted within us the seeds of all the arts and periods of life. And God, our Master, secretly produces our mental dispositions;'

Augustine, On Christian Doctrine. II.18,
https://www.newadvent.org/fathers/12022.htm
Nay, but let every good and true Christian understand that
wherever truth may be found, it belongs to his Master

Calvin, Institutes. II.2.15,
https://www.ccel.org/ccel/calvin/institutes.iv.iii.html
Nay, we cannot read the writings of the ancients on these subjects
without the highest admiration; an admiration which their
excellence will not allow us to withhold. But shall we deem
anything to be noble and praiseworthy, without tracing it to the
hand of God?

If Stoicism and Christianity both agree that all truth is God's truth, and it
becomes the common property of humanity; are we not justified to despoil
the ancient Stoics of various gems of wisdom and to add it to our store?
Jesus himself even commended a Pharisee when he spoke the truth:

Mark 12:34 KJV
And when Jesus saw that he answered discreetly, he said unto him,
Thou art not far from the kingdom of God.

As manly lovers of truth, wherever it may be found, let us embrace the
challenge of differing worldviews, and allow the contest to make us
stronger.

On Advising Others

Who is the true philosopher, and how might we recognize him? Does he have a particular appearance, education, or eloquence of speech? Is he someone who can tell us what to believe or how to live? Rather than someone who puts himself forward to lecture us on how to behave, he should be someone who is showing us a good life by his example.

> Matthew 7:16-18
> Ye shall know them by their fruits. Do men gather grapes of thorns, or figs of thistles? 17 Even so every good tree bringeth forth good fruit; but a corrupt tree bringeth forth evil fruit. 18 A good tree cannot bring forth evil fruit, neither can a corrupt tree bring forth good fruit.

> James 3:13
> Who is a wise man and endued with knowledge among you? let him shew out of a good conversation his works with meekness of wisdom.

> Epictetus, Discourses. 3.13.21
> Practice at one time living like an invalid, so that at another time you can live like a healthy person. Go without food, drink nothing but water, completely abstain at one time from satisfying your appetites, so that at a later time you can satisfy them according to the dictates of reason. If you do that, when the time comes that you have some good in you, your appetites will be good. But no, that's not what we do. We want to live as wise men straightaway, and to help others. But what kind of help could we provide? What

are you up to? Can you help yourself? You want to advise others, but who are you to offer advice? If you want to help others, show them by your example what kind of people philosophy produces, without relying upon empty words. As you eat, help your fellow diners; as you drink, help your fellow drinkers. Yield to others always, give way to them, tolerate them. Help them in this way, not by spattering them with your spit.

Epictetus, Discourses. 3.14.4
When a person drinks nothing but water or adopts some other ascetic practice, he seizes every opportunity to tell everyone about it. 'I drink nothing but water.' What? Is that why you drink only water? Man, if drinking only water does you good, do it. If you do it for any other reason, you're making a fool of yourself. But if it does you good, and you do it, don't talk about it to other people who are irritated by teetotalers. Are these really people you want to please?

Epictetus, Discourses. 4.8.20
And what harm was there in letting my actions rather than any external clues mark me as a philosopher? See how I eat, how I drink, how I sleep, how patient I am, how abstemious, how I help others, how I manage my desires and aversions, how I maintain my social relationships, whether natural or acquired, without confusion or obstruction. Judge me on this basis, if you can.

Before someone can share valuable knowledge with others, he must know it himself in all sincerity and without presumption.

1 Corinthians 8:2

And if any man think that he knoweth any thing, he knoweth nothing yet as he ought to know.

Epictetus, Discourses. 2.17.1
What is the first work for a would-be philosopher to undertake? Eliminating presumption, because it's impossible for anyone to go about learning what he thinks he already knows.

Avoid hypocrisy and condescension toward others. Practice what you preach.

Matthew 7:1-5
Judge not, that ye be not judged. 2 For with what judgment ye judge, ye shall be judged: and with what measure ye mete, it shall be measured to you again. 3 And why beholdest thou the mote that is in thy brother's eye, but considerest not the beam that is in thine own eye? 4 Or how wilt thou say to thy brother, Let me pull out the mote out of thine eye; and, behold, a beam is in thine own eye? 5 Thou hypocrite, first cast out the beam out of thine own eye; and then shalt thou see clearly to cast out the mote out of thy brother's eye.

Romans 2:21-23
Thou therefore which teachest another, teachest thou not thyself? thou that preachest a man should not steal, dost thou steal? 22 Thou that sayest a man should not commit adultery, dost thou commit adultery? thou that abhorrest idols, dost thou commit sacrilege? 23 Thou that makest thy boast of the law, through breaking the law dishonourest thou God?

Seneca, Letters. 27.1

"How is it that you are advising me?" you say. "Have you already advised yourself? Have you got yourself straightened out? Is that why you have the time to correct others?" I am not such a hypocrite as to offer cures while I am sick myself. No, I am lying in the same ward, as it were, conversing with you about our common ailment and sharing remedies.

Aurelius, Meditations. 10.16

Stop all this theorizing about what a good man should be. Be it!

Make a distinction about who you might try to instruct in the way of wisdom. Only share with those who might benefit from it.

Matthew 7:6

Give not that which is holy unto the dogs, neither cast ye your pearls before swine, lest they trample them under their feet, and turn again and rend you.

Jude 1:22-23

And of some have compassion, making a difference: 23 And others save with fear, pulling them out of the fire; hating even the garment spotted by the flesh.

Seneca, Letters. 29.3

An archer ought not to hit the mark sometimes and miss it sometimes: anything that gets its results by chance is not a skill. Wisdom is a skill. It should go after the sure thing, choosing those who will benefit and holding off from those who are beyond hope. Still, it should not abandon them too quickly: desperate cases call for desperate remedies.

Each person is on their own individual journey, and we should focus on our own destination before we try to guide others in the way.

Romans 14:4
Who art thou that judgest another man's servant? to his own master he standeth or falleth. Yea, he shall be holden up: for God is able to make him stand.

Aurelius, Meditations. 5.3
Others have their own consciences to guide them and will follow their own lights. Don't be gazing after them, but keep your eyes on the straight path ahead of you...

Aurelius, Meditations. 10.4
If someone makes a mistake, correct him with kindness and point out where he went wrong. If you fail, blame only yourself, or better yet, don't blame anyone.

Aurelius, Meditations. 10.30
Whenever you are about to find fault with someone, ask yourself the following question: What fault of mine most nearly resembles the one I am about to criticize? Is it the love of money? or pleasure? or reputation? and so on until you have identified the closest cousin. By redirecting your attention in this way, you will soon forget your anger as you realize that he can't help himself any more than you can. How can he possibly overcome the compulsion to do wrong? If you can help him with this, you have helped yourself as well.

On Outwards Shows of Piety

There are those who would take a shortcut to play the part of a learned man, merely adopting outward appearances rather than taking the long road of subjecting oneself to the deprivations of discipline. Jesus criticized the Pharisees for their attention to outward appearance and false shows of piety, while their lives lacked genuine virtue. Stoics also showed distaste for those who would don the philosopher's garb just for appearances, or to embrace statues (it was an ascetic practice to hug a cold statue outdoors, but since statues were often prominently displayed in public places, this was also a real attention-getter).

> Matthew 23:5-7
> But all their works they do for to be seen of men: they make broad their phylacteries, and enlarge the borders of their garments, 6 And love the uppermost rooms at feasts, and the chief seats in the synagogues, 7 And greetings in the markets, and to be called of men, Rabbi, Rabbi.

> John 5:44
> How can ye believe, which receive honour one of another, and seek not the honour that cometh from God only?

> Seneca, Letters. 5.1
> There are those whose wish is to be noticed rather than to make moral progress. Don't be like them, altering your dress or way of life so as to attract attention.

> Seneca, Letters. 113.32

People who want their virtue to be advertised are working for renown rather than virtue. Aren't you willing to be just without renown? In fact, of course, you will often have to combine being just with being disgraced. And then if you are wise, you should take delight in the bad reputation you have won by your good behavior.

Epictetus, Handbook. 47
When you've become accustomed to reducing your bodily needs, don't flaunt it. If you're a teetotaler, don't seize every opportunity to let people know that you're a teetotaler. If you want to train yourself to endure physical hardship, do so for yourself, not for others. Don't hug statues! Instead, when you're parched with thirst, take cold water into your mouth and spit it out again-without telling anyone.

Aurelius, Meditations. 3.4
He attaches no importance whatsoever to the praise of these men, who can find no reason to praise themselves.

Aurelius, Meditations. 12.2
God sees the minds of men stripped of their material shells and husks and impurities. With his pure intellect, he touches the very parts that flowed from him into ourselves. Make a habit of doing the same and you will rid yourself of most distractions. Will the man who ignores his fleshly shell waste time fussing with his dress, his dwelling, his popularity- the costumes and stage scenery of life?

Virtue is its own reward. If you do good deeds in the pursuit of virtue, do not make a public display of it for the sake of notoriety. There is no shortcut to genuine virtue, short of hypocrisy.

Matthew 6:1-4

Take heed that ye do not your alms before men, to be seen of them: otherwise ye have no reward of your Father which is in heaven. 2 Therefore when thou doest thine alms, do not sound a trumpet before thee, as the hypocrites do in the synagogues and in the streets, that they may have glory of men. Verily I say unto you, They have their reward. 3 But when thou doest alms, let not thy left hand know what thy right hand doeth: 4 That thine alms may be in secret: and thy Father which seeth in secret himself shall reward thee openly.

Matthew 6:5-6

And when thou prayest, thou shalt not be as the hypocrites are: for they love to pray standing in the synagogues and in the corners of the streets, that they may be seen of men. Verily I say unto you, They have their reward. 6 But thou, when thou prayest, enter into thy closet, and when thou hast shut thy door, pray to thy Father which is in secret; and thy Father which seeth in secret shall reward thee openly.

Matthew 6:16-18

Moreover when ye fast, be not, as the hypocrites, of a sad countenance: for they disfigure their faces, that they may appear unto men to fast. Verily I say unto you, They have their reward. 17 But thou, when thou fastest, anoint thine head, and wash thy face; 18 That thou appear not unto men to fast, but unto thy Father which is in secret: and thy Father, which seeth in secret, shall reward thee openly.

Seneca, Letters. 79.18

In life or in death, the pursuit of virtue never goes unrewarded, as long as one has followed it in earnest, not with hairstyle and makeup but with a character that is the same on the surprise visit as on the planned occasion. Pretense is of no avail. Few are deceived by the face that is just painted on: one's true identity goes right to the core. Deceits have nothing about them. A lie is a tenuous thing, and on close inspection, transparent.

Aurelius, Meditations. 4.20

Praise adds nothing to beauty- makes it neither better nor worse. This is also true for commonly praised objects, natural wonders, for example, or works of art. What does anything that is truly beautiful lack? Nothing! No more than does natural law, truth, kindness, or self-respect. Which of these is improved by praise or marred by criticism?

Aurelius, Meditations. 7.73

When you have done something well and someone else has benefitted from it, why do you crave yet a third reward, as fools do, who want to be thanked or to be repaid?

Aurelius, Meditations. 9.42

Having done a good deed, what more do you want? Isn't it enough to have acted in harmony with your nature? Do you need to be paid for it as well? Do the eyes demand payment for seeing, or the feet wages for walking? Just as these organs were made for what they do and find fulfillment in doing what they were made to do, so too are men made by nature for one another. Whenever they perform a good deed or contribute to the common good in some way, they do what they were made to do and receive all that is theirs.

Jesus elucidated on this point of how genuine character should be dutifully attentive to pleasing God at all times, and so should be the same on a surprise visit as on a planned occasion. Good works should be done in virtuous obedience, and not in seeking a reward in the accolades of others.

Luke 12:35-40

Let your loins be girded about, and your lights burning; 36 And ye yourselves like unto men that wait for their lord, when he will return from the wedding; that when he cometh and knocketh, they may open unto him immediately. 37 Blessed are those servants, whom the lord when he cometh shall find watching: verily I say unto you, that he shall gird himself, and make them to sit down to meat, and will come forth and serve them. 38 And if he shall come in the second watch, or come in the third watch, and find them so, blessed are those servants. 39 And this know, that if the goodman of the house had known what hour the thief would come, he would have watched, and not have suffered his house to be broken through. 40 Be ye therefore ready also: for the Son of man cometh at an hour when ye think not.

Luke 17:7-10

But which of you, having a servant plowing or feeding cattle, will say unto him by and by, when he is come from the field, Go and sit down to meat? 8 And will not rather say unto him, Make ready wherewith I may sup, and gird thyself, and serve me, till I have eaten and drunken; and afterward thou shalt eat and drink? 9 Doth he thank that servant because he did the things that were commanded him? I trow not. 10 So likewise ye, when ye shall have done all those things which are commanded you, say, We are unprofitable servants: we have done that which was our duty to do.

Genuine virtue is something that flows naturally from the inside. There should not be a disconnect between what is, and what is professed or what is seen by others. Pretense is useless, and the praises of other men are vain and meaningless. God sees into the secrets of the heart, and all that we think, say and do is in his audience.

Matthew 12:33-35
Either make the tree good, and his fruit good; or else make the tree corrupt, and his fruit corrupt: for the tree is known by his fruit. 34 O generation of vipers, how can ye, being evil, speak good things? for out of the abundance of the heart the mouth speaketh. 35 A good man out of the good treasure of the heart bringeth forth good things: and an evil man out of the evil treasure bringeth forth evil things.

Hebrews 4:12-13
For the word of God is quick, and powerful, and sharper than any twoedged sword, piercing even to the dividing asunder of soul and spirit, and of the joints and marrow, and is a discerner of the thoughts and intents of the heart. 13 Neither is there any creature that is not manifest in his sight: but all things are naked and opened unto the eyes of him with whom we have to do.

Seneca, Letters. 10.5
Consider whether the following may not be a healthful bit of advice: live with humans as if God may be watching; speak with God as if humans may be listening.

Seneca, Letters. 83.1

Our lives should indeed be like that, lived as in the sight of others. Even our thoughts should be conducted as though some other person could gaze into our inmost breast. For there is someone who can. What use is there in keeping a secret from human beings? Nothing is hidden from God. God is in our minds; God enters into the midst of our thoughts. I say *enters*– as if he had ever left!

Rufus, Lectures. 5.4

...in the matter of temperance and self-control, is it not much better to be self-controlled and temperate in all one's actions than to be able to say what one ought to do?

Rufus, Lectures. 6.2

How, indeed, could a person immediately become temperate if he only knew that one must not be overcome by pleasures, but was quite unpracticed in withstanding pleasures? How could one become just when he had learned that one must love fairness but had never exercised himself in avoidance of selfishness and greed? How could we acquire courage if we had merely learned that the things which seem dreadful to the average person are not to be feared, but had no experience in showing courage in the face of such things? How could we become prudent if we had come to recognize what things are truly good and what evil, but had never had practice in despising things which only seem good?

Epictetus, Discourses. 2.14.11

The philosophers say that the first thing we need to understand is that God exists, that he cares providentially for the universe, and that it's impossible for us to conceal from him not just our actions but our intentions and thoughts as well.

Aurelius, Meditations. 4.3

Or are you tormented by what others may think of you? Look then on how soon everything is forgotten, and gaze into the abyss of infinite time. Hear the hollowness of the applause, and ponder the fickleness of those who are applauding you while you consider the narrowness of the stage on which you pant after their plaudits. The entire earth is but a piece of dust blowing through the firmament, and the inhabited part of the earth a small fraction thereof. So, in such a grand space, how many do you think will think of you, and what will their thoughts be worth?

Aurelius, Meditations. 4.18

How much time and effort a man saves by paying no attention to what his neighbor says or does or thinks, and by concentrating on his own behavior to make it holy and just! The good man isn't looking around for cheaters. He dashes straight for the finish and leans into the tape.

On Enduring Insult

A man of virtue should not be swayed by what others think of him, whether it be to seek their praise or to avoid their reproach. To bear insult and even injury unflinchingly is the mark of true fortitude. It should be received as a means of discipline.

Matthew 5:11
Blessed are ye, when men shall revile you, and persecute you, and shall say all manner of evil against you falsely, for my sake.

Matthew 5:39
39 But I say unto you, That ye resist not evil: but whosoever shall smite thee on thy right cheek, turn to him the other also.

1 Peter 2:23
Who, when he was reviled, reviled not again; when he suffered, he threatened not; but committed himself to him that judgeth righteously:

Rufus, Lectures. 10.2-5
For actually none of the things which people fancy they suffer as personal injuries are an injury or a disgrace to those who experience them, such as being reviled or struck or spit upon. Of these the hardest to bear are blows. That there is nothing shameful or insulting about them however is clear from the fact that Lacedaemonian boys are whipped publicly, and they exult in it. If, then, the philosopher cannot despise blows and insults when he ought obviously to despise even death, what good would he be?

Epictetus, Handbook. 50

Stick with every goal you set yourself as you would abide by laws–
that is, regarding it as wicked to transgress any of them. Don't
worry about what people will say about you, because that's no
longer your business.

Epictetus, Discourses. 3.12.10

Man, if you have the grit, train yourself to put up with abuse and
not get angry if you're insulted. And then you'll make such
progress that, even if someone punches you, you'll tell yourself to
imagine that you're hugging a statue.

Epictetus, Discourses. 3.13.17

'But what if someone assaults me when I'm alone and murders
me?' Fool, that's not you, but your body.

Epictetus, Discourses. 3.20.9

What does an athlete gain from his training partner? A very great
deal. So someone who insults me is training me up. He gives me
practice in tolerance, in not losing my temper, in being
mild-mannered. You disagree? But if it does me good to have
someone grab me by the neck and for him to get my loins and
shoulders into shape, and if the trainer is right to ask me for a
two-handed lift of the pestle, and the heavier the pestle, the more I
am benefited, then doesn't someone do me good if he trains me in
not losing my temper?

Epictetus, Discourses. 3.22.100-102

A Cynic must be a person of such great endurance that ordinary people take him to be unfeeling as a stone. No one can insult him, no one can hit him, no one can humiliate him. Any way that anyone wants to treat his body is all right with him, because he bears in mind that what is superior is bound to prevail over what is inferior, in the respect in which it's inferior, and that his body is necessarily inferior to the mass of ordinary people, as the weaker is to the stronger. So he never gets involved in this contest, which he can only lose, but instead completely renounces everything that's external to him and claims nothing that's enslaved as his own.

Epictetus, Discourses. 4.5.9

'So-and-so railed at me.' I'm very grateful to him for not hitting me. 'But he hit me as well.' I'm very grateful that he didn't injure me. 'But he injured me as well.' I'm very grateful that he didn't kill me.

Epictetus, Discourses. 4.5.11-12

'My neighbor has thrown stones.' It's not you who has done wrong, then, is it? 'But some things in my house were broken.' Well, are you one of your domestic utensils? No, you are a will. So what means have you been given to respond to this situation? If you react like a wolf, you'll bite him back and throw a greater number of stones in your turn. But if you want to react like a human being, examine your resources and see what faculties you were born with. Was ferocity one of them? Was vindictiveness?

Epictetus, Discourses. 4.5.22-23

"What? Do you want me to be despised?"

"By whom? By knowledgeable people? How could knowledgeable people despise someone who's gentle and has self-respect? By ignorant people? Why would you care? I mean, no craftsman cares what people who are ignorant of his craft think of him."

"But they'll pester me all the more."

"Why do you say 'me'?" Can anyone damage your will or prevent you from making natural use of the impressions that occur to you?"

Aurelius, Meditations. 7.22

It is within a man's power to love even those who sin against him. This becomes possible when you realize that they are your brothers, that they wrong you unintentionally or out of ignorance, that in a little while you and they will be dead, and above all, they have not really hurt you so long as you have not sullied your conscience or damaged your inner self by responding in kind.

Aurelius, Meditations. 9.31

When facing whatever happens outside your control, be calm; when taking actions for which you are responsible, be fair. In other words, whether acting or reacting, your aim is the aid and betterment of others, in fulfillment of nature's laws.

Aurelius, Meditations. 10.13

From the moment that you wake up, ask yourself: Does it really matter if someone criticizes my correct and just acts? Not at all.

On Suffering Persecution

Persecution is to be endured virtuously, with trust that God is in control, and that he allows it to happen to you for a good purpose.

Matthew 5:10
Blessed are they which are persecuted for righteousness' sake: for theirs is the kingdom of heaven.

Romans 8:28
And we know that all things work together for good to them that love God, to them who are the called according to his purpose.

1 Peter 4:19
Wherefore let them that suffer according to the will of God commit the keeping of their souls to him in well doing, as unto a faithful Creator.

Aurelius, Meditations. 4.10
"Whatever happens happens justly." Pay close attention and you will see that this is so. By this I don't mean only that justice will result from whatever happens, but I mean that a just purpose will also be served, as is the case when payment is made for work or prizes are awarded for victory. So be particularly scrupulous in this, and continue as you have begun, a decent man performing every deed conscious of the most rigorous requirements of goodness. Preserve this sense in every act.

Aurelius, Meditations. 4.39

You cannot be harmed by the law of another man's being, nor can any change or alteration in your circumstances hurt you. Where is the injury then? It is in your sense of injury- in the part of you that forms a judgment about such things. Form no judgment, and the injury disappears. Even if what is closest to you, your body, is mutilated and burned, festers and rots, force the part of you that forms an opinion about such things to remain calm and refuse to judge as either good or bad what can as easily happen to a good man as to a bad.

Aurelius, Meditations. 5.8
Accept the prescriptions of nature as if they were intended for your own health, even if at times they may seem cruel or disagreeable to you. Remember that they are for the good of the universe and for the pleasure of God. Nothing is prescribed for any part that does not benefit the whole. After all, it would violate the nature of anything to act against its own interests in governing its parts. There are two reasons, then, for being content with whatever happens to you. The first is that it was meant just for you, prescribed for you, and preserved for you like a thread woven into your destiny from the very beginning. The second is that whatever happens to the individual contributes to the health, wholeness, and survival of the entire universe.

Aurelius, Meditations. 8.48
You will recall how impregnable your mind is when it withdraws into itself and steadfastly refuses to do what it doesn't want to do, even when refusal is unreasonable. Imagine then what it's like when it arrives at a decision calmly and reasonably. Free from passions, the mind is a veritable fortress. A man cannot find a more

secure place to take refuge and remain unassailable forever. Ignorant is he who fails to see this, and truly ill-fated is he who sees but fails to take refuge.

Aurelius, Meditations. 8.51

So what if they kill you, hack you to pieces, hunt you down with curses. How can this keep your mind from being pure, sound, temperate, and just? If a man were to stop beside a limpid spring of sweet water and start hurling insults at it, would it suddenly cease to flow? Even if he threw mud and excrement into the stream, it would soon dissolve and wash away and leave not taint or stain. How then can you possess an ever-flowing stream? By using the freedom you already possess to imbue your character with compassion, simplicity, modesty.

On Suffering Loss

To rise above the fleeting and transitory things of this life, the wise man must realize that he does not possess anything as his own to keep forever. We must soon release all things when we pass from this life, so there is no real harm in relinquishing something a little earlier. If something is taken from us, we can let go of it without remorse. Though we may sway momentarily with feeling at the pain of loss, it should not harm our core being.

> Matthew 5:40-42
> And if any man will sue thee at the law, and take away thy coat, let him have thy cloke also. 41 And whosoever shall compel thee to go a mile, go with him twain. 42 Give to him that asketh thee, and from him that would borrow of thee turn not thou away.

> Romans 12:15
> Rejoice with them that do rejoice, and weep with them that weep.

> 1 Corinthians 7:29-31
> But this I say, brethren, the time is short: it remaineth, that both they that have wives be as though they had none; 30 And they that weep, as though they wept not; and they that rejoice, as though they rejoiced not; and they that buy, as though they possessed not; 31 And they that use this world, as not abusing it: for the fashion of this world passeth away.

Seneca, Letters. 42.10

Once a person possesses himself, then nothing is ever lost to him.

Epictetus, Handbook. 11

Never say, "I've lost it" about anything, but "I've returned it." Has your child died? It has been returned. Has your wife died? She has been returned. Has your estate been confiscated? So that too has been returned. "But the person who confiscated it is a bad man." What difference does it make to you whom the donor used as the agent of its return? As long as they're in your charge, treat them as things that belong to someone else, as travelers treat an inn.

Epictetus, Handbook. 16

Whenever you see someone weeping out of grief for the departure of a child or because he's lost some property, make sure you don't get carried away by the impression that his external circumstances really are bad. Instead, have at hand the reminder that "It's not what's happened that's distressing him (otherwise it would distress everyone), but his judgment about what's happened." Don't hesitate, however, to sympathize with him verbally, and even to mourn along with him, if that is what the occasion calls for. But make sure that you do not mourn inwardly as well.

Epictetus, Discourses. 1.24.14

Have I forgotten that none of these things is mine? The only sense in which they're mine, then, is the sense in which we say that a bed at an inn is mine.

Aurelius, Meditations. 10.14

To nature, the giver and taker of all things, the wise and self-respecting man says, "Give what is your pleasure to give; take what you will." This he says, not in a tone of swaggering machismo, but in an attentive and obedient voice.

Aurelius, Meditations. 12.26

You can claim nothing as your own. Your child, your body, your very soul come from God. Finally, you're forgetting that everything is what your opinion makes it and that the present moment is all you have, to live and lose.

On Transitory Living

The wise man should not cling to life in this world, but dispose himself in a perpetual state of readiness to depart; like a traveler who is ready to move on, or a servant who is merely watching over the affairs of his master.

Luke 12:35-40
Let your loins be girded about, and your lights burning; 36 And ye yourselves like unto men that wait for their lord, when he will return from the wedding; that when he cometh and knocketh, they may open unto him immediately. 37 Blessed are those servants, whom the lord when he cometh shall find watching: verily I say unto you, that he shall gird himself, and make them to sit down to meat, and will come forth and serve them. 38 And if he shall come in the second watch, or come in the third watch, and find them so, blessed are those servants. 39 And this know, that if the goodman of the house had known what hour the thief would come, he would have watched, and not have suffered his house to be broken through. 40 Be ye therefore ready also: for the Son of man cometh at an hour when ye think not.

Epictetus, Handbook. 7
Suppose you're traveling by sea and the boat puts in somewhere, and you disembark to get some water. While you're at it you might also pick up a bit of shellfish and a few bulbs, but you have to keep your mind fixed on the boat and pay constant attention in case the captain calls you back, and, if the call comes, you have to leave all those things behind to avoid being tied up and hoisted on board like the sheep. The same goes for life too. Suppose you've been

given, not bulbs and shellfish, but a wife and child. All well and good, but if the captain calls, run to the boat, leaving all those things behind, without paying them any mind. And, if you're elderly, you also shouldn't ever stray far from the boat, in case the call comes and you get left behind.

The wise man does not cling to the goods of this life, nor does he reflexively thrust them away; he can live harmoniously with or without them. There were occasions where Jesus was honored and invited to banquets, and other times where he was despised and went hungry. He was able to deal with any situation.

Philippians 4:11-13
Not that I speak in respect of want: for I have learned, in whatsoever state I am, therewith to be content. 12 I know both how to be abased, and I know how to abound: every where and in all things I am instructed both to be full and to be hungry, both to abound and to suffer need. 13 I can do all things through Christ which strengtheneth me.

Seneca, Letters. 5.6
A person entering our house should marvel at the inhabitant, not at the dinnerware. One who uses earthenware as if it were silver is indeed a great person; equally great, though, is the one who uses silver as if it were earthenware. Not being able to cope with wealth is an indication of weakness.

Seneca, Letters. 18.13
No one is worthy of God unless he has risen above wealth. I do not forbid you to possess wealth; I only seek to make you fearless in

possessing it. And the only way to achieve that is if you convince yourself that you will be happy even without it- if you look at it as something that might disappear at any moment.

Seneca, Letters. 74.18
May all those things come to us, but may they not cling to us; so that if they should be taken away, their departure will not tear us apart. Let us use them, not glory in them; and let us use them sparingly, as loans that will someday be recalled.

Ever conscious of the transitory nature of this life, we cannot assure ourselves of future circumstances in this world, which are never certain.

James 4:13-14
Go to now, ye that say, To day or to morrow we will go into such a city, and continue there a year, and buy and sell, and get gain: 14 Whereas ye know not what shall be on the morrow. For what is your life? It is even a vapour, that appeareth for a little time, and then vanisheth away.

Seneca, Letters. 101.4-5
How foolish it is to plan out one's life when one is not even the master of tomorrow! What madness it is to undertake lengthy projects, saying: "I will buy and build, I will make loans and demand them back, I will hold public offices, and then I will retire to enjoy a long and leisurely old age." Everything is uncertain, believe me, even for those who are fortunate. No one should make himself any promises concerning the future.

Seneca, Letters. 101.15

What matters is not how long you live but how well. And often, living well consists in not living long.

Seneca, Letters. 120.14

That heart is at its most divine when it reflects on its own mortality. Then it knows that a human being is born in order to complete life's term with a body that is not a home but a sort of short-term guesthouse- something you have to leave when you see that you are becoming bothersome to your host.

Seneca, Letters. 120.18

So a great mind, cognizant of its better nature, makes a real effort to behave honorably and assiduously in the position where it has been placed, but it does not regard any of its surroundings as its own. It uses them as things it has been lent, like a traveler who is moving on.

Aurelius, Meditations. 3.10

Little of life we know, little the plot of earth on which we dwell, little the memory of even the most famous who have lived, and this memory itself is preserved by generations of little men, who know little about themselves and far less about those who died long ago.

Aurelius, Meditations. 3.12

...if you keep your divine spirit pure and blameless, as though this were the moment to give it back...

On Living in the Present

The wise man should not fret over the past nor worry about the future, but maintain a tranquil disposition of mind through focus on the present day.

Matthew 6:34
Take therefore no thought for the morrow: for the morrow shall take thought for the things of itself. Sufficient unto the day is the evil thereof.

Seneca, Letters. 5.9
Animals in the wild flee the dangers they see and are tranquil once they have escaped; we, though, are tormented both by what is to come and by what has been. Often, our goods do us harm: memory recalls the stab of fear; foresight anticipates it. No one is made wretched merely by the present.

Seneca, Letters. 13.7
"How am I to know," you say, "whether the causes of my anxiety are real or empty?" Here is your measuring stick. We are tormented either by things past, or by things to come, or both. Concerning things present it is easy to make a judgment: if your body is at liberty, and healthy, if you are not in pain from any injury, then we can wait and see what is to come; today is not an issue.

Seneca, Letters. 78.14
There are two things, then, that one ought to cut back: fear of future troubles and memories of those that are past. One concerns me no longer, the other not yet.

Seneca, Letters. 92.25

The special quality of virtue is that it has no need of the future and does not count its own days. In a mere instant, it enjoys eternal blessings.

Seneca, Letters. 94.7

Just as one of small stature can be a complete human being, so too a life of less duration can be complete. Age is something external. How long I am to exist does not belong to me; what is mine is authentic existence. This you can demand of me- that I not measure out a humdrum age in obscurity; that I live my life, not pass it by.

Aurelius, Meditations. 3.10

We live only in the present, in this fleet-footed moment. The rest is lost behind us, or ahead of us and may never be found.

Aurelius, Meditations. 4.45

What follows always bears some relation to what came before. Life is not like an arbitrary series of random numbers, but more like a logical progression. Likewise, just as natural objects appear to cooperate and exist in harmony with one another, so too events are not remarkable because of the order in which they happen, but because of their amazing affinity with one another.

Aurelius, Meditations. 6.37

If you have seen the present, you have seen everything that was and all that will be, world without end; for it all rises from the same source and takes the same form.

Aurelius, Meditations. 7.69

To live each day as if it were your last without speeding up or slowing down or pretending to be other than what you are- this is perfection of character.

Aurelius, Meditations. 8.44

Give yourself the present. Those who chase after future fame fail to realize that the men whose praise they crave tomorrow will be no different from the men whose opinions they despise today, and all these men will die. What do you care whether tomorrow's men know the sound of your name or say nice things about you?

On Anxiety

Anxiety over possible future misfortune is misguided and unproductive. We should focus on the present moment which has been given to us, and trust the future (which we cannot control) to divine providence.

Luke 12:25-26
And which of you with taking thought can add to his stature one cubit? 26 If ye then be not able to do that thing which is least, why take ye thought for the rest?

Philippians 4:6-8
Be careful for nothing; but in every thing by prayer and supplication with thanksgiving let your requests be made known unto God. 7 And the peace of God, which passeth all understanding, shall keep your hearts and minds through Christ Jesus. 8 Finally, brethren, whatsoever things are true, whatsoever things are honest, whatsoever things are just, whatsoever things are pure, whatsoever things are lovely, whatsoever things are of good report; if there be any virtue, and if there be any praise, think on these things.

1 Peter 5:7
Casting all your care upon him; for he careth for you.

Seneca, Letters. 74.30
All anxiety and worry is dishonorable, all reluctance to act; for honorable conduct is sure and unhampered, undismayed, ever standing at the ready.

Seneca, Letters. 74.32

But when foolishness has something to fear, it is as tormented in its expectation as though the bad thing had already occurred: what it fears to endure, it endures already through fear.

Seneca, Letters. 82.4

What's to be gained by getting away from it all? As if our worries won't follow us across the sea! What retreat is there where the fear of death cannot enter? What quiet spot, in the deepest mountain stronghold, that is not made fearsome by the thought of pain? No matter where you hide, you will be surrounded by the hue and cry of human misfortune. All around us are external cares to deceive and oppress us; many more come boiling up from within, even in the midst of solitude.

Seneca, Letters. 98.6

A mind that is anxious about the future and unhappy before misfortune even arrives is a disaster, concerned that the things it delights in should last forever. It will never be in repose, and in its anticipation of what is to come it will lose the present things that it could enjoy. The fear of losing something is equivalent to the pain of its loss.

On The Fear of Poverty

A common cause of anxiety is due to a tenuous grasping of worldly wealth and a fear of not having enough for one's needs in the future. Maintaining a perspective that rests secure in divine providence and also looks beyond the transitory things of this life is the only way to maintain true security.

> Luke 12:22-34
> And he said unto his disciples, Therefore I say unto you, Take no thought for your life, what ye shall eat; neither for the body, what ye shall put on. 23 The life is more than meat, and the body is more than raiment. 24 Consider the ravens: for they neither sow nor reap; which neither have storehouse nor barn; and God feedeth them: how much more are ye better than the fowls? 25 And which of you with taking thought can add to his stature one cubit? 26 If ye then be not able to do that thing which is least, why take ye thought for the rest? 27 Consider the lilies how they grow: they toil not, they spin not; and yet I say unto you, that Solomon in all his glory was not arrayed like one of these. 28 If then God so clothe the grass, which is to day in the field, and to morrow is cast into the oven; how much more will he clothe you, O ye of little faith? 29 And seek not ye what ye shall eat, or what ye shall drink, neither be ye of doubtful mind. 30 For all these things do the nations of the world seek after: and your Father knoweth that ye have need of these things. 31 But rather seek ye the kingdom of God; and all these things shall be added unto you.

Luke 10:7

And in the same house remain, eating and drinking such things as they give: for the labourer is worthy of his hire.

Rufus, Lectures. 15.2-3

... I am a poor man and quite without means, and if I have many children, from what source should I find food for them all? But pray, whence do the little birds, which are much poorer than you, feed their young, the swallows and nightingales and larks and blackbirds? Homer speaks of them in these words:

> Even as a bird carries to her unfledged young whatever
> morsels she happens to come upon, though she fares badly
> herself-

Do these creatures surpass man in intelligence? You certainly would not say that. In strength and endurance, then? No, still less in that respect. Well, then, do they put away food and store it up? Not at all, and yet they rear their young and find sustenance for all that are born to them. The plea of poverty, therefore, is unjustified.

Epictetus, Discourses. 1.9.8-9

"And where am I to get food from," someone asked, "if I have nothing?"

"Well, how do slaves eat, runaways? What do they rely on when they leave their masters? On their fields, their servants, their silverware? No, they rely on nothing but themselves, but they don't go short of food. Will our philosopher, when he's away from home, have to trust and depend on others, rather than take care of himself? Will he be more craven and cowardly than the non-rational creatures of the wild, every one of which is self-sufficient and doesn't go without either its proper food or the way of life that suits it and accords with its nature?

Epictetus, Discourses. 3.26.1-2

Doesn't it make you ashamed to be more cowardly and base than runaway slaves? When they run off and leave their masters, how do they manage? What farms and slaves do they rely on? Don't they purloin a few supplies, enough for the first few days, and then afterward, wherever they go by land or sea, devise one ingenious way after another to keep themselves in food? And what runaway slave ever died of hunger? But you're so frightened of running out of the means of sustenance that you can't sleep at night.

Epictetus, Discourses. 3.26.27-28

Is anyone good afraid of running out of food? The blind don't run out of food, nor do the lame, so a good person won't either, will he? A good soldier never fails to find someone to pay him, nor does a good laborer or cobbler, so a good person won't wither, will he? Is God that neglectful of his prize exhibits- his servants, his witnesses, the only people he can use as examples for the uneducated, to show that he exists, that his governance of the universe is good, that he doesn't neglect human affairs, and that nothing bad happens to a good person either during his lifetime or after his death?

Aurelius, Meditations. 7.8

Don't fear the future. You will face it, if that is your fate, armed with the same reason that protects and guides you in the present.

Aurelius, Meditations. 9.32

Many of the things that trouble you are easily disposed of, for they are all in your mind. Instead of dwelling on them in such cramped quarters, why not inhabit spacious chambers by taking into your mind the whole wide world, the vast expanse of eternity, the swift succession of change in the smallest parts of everything.

On Storing Wealth

It is a common aspiration to gain stores of wealth as a kind of security against the future, but this is something which it can never provide; for not only can your riches be easily taken from you, but you can be easily taken from your riches– when you depart this life.

Matthew 6:19-21
Lay not up for yourselves treasures upon earth, where moth and rust doth corrupt, and where thieves break through and steal: 20 But lay up for yourselves treasures in heaven, where neither moth nor rust doth corrupt, and where thieves do not break through nor steal: 21 For where your treasure is, there will your heart be also.

Luke 12:16-21
And he spake a parable unto them, saying, The ground of a certain rich man brought forth plentifully: 17 And he thought within himself, saying, What shall I do, because I have no room where to bestow my fruits? 18 And he said, This will I do: I will pull down my barns, and build greater; and there will I bestow all my fruits and my goods. 19 And I will say to my soul, Soul, thou hast much goods laid up for many years; take thine ease, eat, drink, and be merry. 20 But God said unto him, Thou fool, this night thy soul shall be required of thee: then whose shall those things be, which thou hast provided? 21 So is he that layeth up treasure for himself, and is not rich toward God.

Seneca, Letters. 45.9

His goods are those no power can strip away; whatever is bad, he turns to good.

Seneca, Letters. 87.7

[Speaking of a rich man...]

He is a poor man all the same. Why? Because he is in debt. "How much does he owe?" you ask. Everything! Or do you perhaps think that owing one's goods to fortune is somehow different from owing a human creditor?

Seneca, Letters. 89.21

Yet when you have done so much enormous building, you still have only one body apiece, and that a puny one. What good are numerous bedrooms? You can only lie in one of them. Any place you do not occupy is not really yours.

Fortune seeks to conquer the human will, either through deprivation or luxury. If it cannot break someone through pain, it entices them with pleasure. If it cannot terrorize someone with poverty, it seduces them with wealth. Either way, through misery or enjoyment, fortune assails the tranquility of the free mind. Would it be bliss to gain a situation where you no longer have to work for a living? This is not a good thing, but is in itself a debilitating weakness. If your security is in your wealth, you are in the least secure position of all.

Seneca, Letters. 55.1

Soft living punishes us with weakness: after refusing to do a thing for some time, we cease to be able to do it.

Seneca, Letters. 87.32

Good things ought properly to be blameless. Goods are pure: they do not corrupt the mind, do not cause anxiety; they elevate and expand the mind but without conceit. Goods inspire confidence, riches inspire audacity; goods produce greatness of spirit, riches produce extravagance, which is nothing but a false show of greatness.

Seneca, Letters. 124.24

Do not judge yourself to be happy until all your joys arise from yourself, until, after viewing the objects of human competition, covetousness, and possessiveness, you find- I will not say nothing to prefer, but nothing to set your heart on. I will give you a brief rule by which to measure yourself, to gauge when you have achieved perfection: you will possess your own good when you understand that the fortunate are really the least fortunate of all.

On Covetousness

When faced with a question by someone about being deprived of an inheritance, Jesus declines to get involved with something that is not his problem; and then he reframes the issue away from getting one's fair share, to living a life devoid of the desire for an abundance of possessions. The fundamental problem is not one of externals, but one of internal disposition.

> Luke 12:13-15
> And one of the company said unto him, Master, speak to my brother, that he divide the inheritance with me. 14 And he said unto him, Man, who made me a judge or a divider over you? 15 And he said unto them, Take heed, and beware of covetousness: for a man's life consisteth not in the abundance of the things which he possesseth.

> Epictetus, Discourses. 3.3.8-10
> However, if we locate goodness in the correct use of will, maintaining one's relationships becomes a good, and moreover, it's a good that one gains by giving up some externals. 'My father's taking away my money.' But he's not harming you. 'My brother's getting more of the estate.' Let him have all he wants. He won't be getting your self-respect, your trustworthiness, or your brotherly love, will he? Who can make you part with these possessions?

> Seneca, Letters. 2.6
> Indeed, it is not poverty if it is cheerful: the pauper is not the person who has too little but the one who desires more. What does

it matter how much is stashed in his strongbox or in his warehouses, how much he has in livestock or interest income, if he hangs on another's possessions, computing not what has been gained but what there is yet to gain? Do you ask what is the limit of wealth? Having what one needs, first of all; then, having enough.

Seneca, Letters. 39.4
Greatness of spirit despises great wealth; it prefers moderate means to abundance. For moderation is useful and life-giving, while abundance harms a person through excess. It is like a yield of wheat that is so heavy it flattens the stalks; like a load of fruit that breaks the branches; like livestock that bear too many young for all to reach maturity. That happens with minds too when they are spoiled by immoderate prosperity, which they use to the detriment of others and even to their own.

Aurelius, Meditations. 7.27
Don't hanker after what you don't have. Instead, fix your attentions on the finest and best that you have, and imagine how much you would long for these if they weren't in your possession. At the same time, don't become so attached to these things that you would be distraught if you were to lose them.

The wealth that we have, we should regard not as our own, but as something we manage as a steward in trust for our master. The wise steward is not the one who does everything he can to preserve and increase holdings under any circumstance, but the one who realizes that it will soon be taken from him, and that the only way he can truly advantage himself for the long term is to dispense with wealth in such a way that secures the greater good of human relationships.

Luke 16:1-13

And he said also unto his disciples, There was a certain rich man, which had a steward; and the same was accused unto him that he had wasted his goods. 2 And he called him, and said unto him, How is it that I hear this of thee? give an account of thy stewardship; for thou mayest be no longer steward. 3 Then the steward said within himself, What shall I do? for my lord taketh away from me the stewardship: I cannot dig; to beg I am ashamed. 4 I am resolved what to do, that, when I am put out of the stewardship, they may receive me into their houses. 5 So he called every one of his lord's debtors unto him, and said unto the first, How much owest thou unto my lord? 6 And he said, An hundred measures of oil. And he said unto him, Take thy bill, and sit down quickly, and write fifty. 7 Then said he to another, And how much owest thou? And he said, An hundred measures of wheat. And he said unto him, Take thy bill, and write fourscore. 8 And the lord commended the unjust steward, because he had done wisely: for the children of this world are in their generation wiser than the children of light. 9 And I say unto you, Make to yourselves friends of the mammon of unrighteousness; that, when ye fail, they may receive you into everlasting habitations. 10 He that is faithful in that which is least is faithful also in much: and he that is unjust in the least is unjust also in much. 11 If therefore ye have not been faithful in the unrighteous mammon, who will commit to your trust the true riches? 12 And if ye have not been faithful in that which is another man's, who shall give you that which is your own? 13 No servant can serve two masters: for either he will hate the one, and love the other; or else he will hold to the one, and despise the other. Ye cannot serve God and mammon.

On Contentment

The objective of living a good life is to attain a state of well-being and happiness based upon virtuous living. Fundamental to this objective is being content with one's lot in life, and not going astray by pining after external things that one might lack, or coveting what others have. Contentment is relative to an internal disposition of gratitude, such that those who have little can be content with simply meeting their basic needs, while those who have much can be unhappily fixated on gaining ever more riches. To possess one's soul in tranquility is more than to possess the whole external world.

> Matthew 16:26
> For what is a man profited, if he shall gain the whole world, and lose his own soul? or what shall a man give in exchange for his soul?

> 1 Timothy 6:6-10
> But godliness with contentment is great gain. 7 For we brought nothing into this world, and it is certain we can carry nothing out. 8 And having food and raiment let us be therewith content. 9 But they that will be rich fall into temptation and a snare, and into many foolish and hurtful lusts, which drown men in destruction and perdition. 10 For the love of money is the root of all evil: which while some coveted after, they have erred from the faith, and pierced themselves through with many sorrows.

Hebrews 13:5

Let your conversation be without covetousness; and be content with such things as ye have: for he hath said, I will never leave thee, nor forsake thee.

Seneca, Letters. 4.10-11

Do you know what boundaries nature's law imposes? Not to be hungry, not to be thirsty, not to be cold. To keep back hunger and thirst, you need not hang about the thresholds of the proud, nor endure the scorn of those whose very kindness is insulting; you need not brave the seas nor follow the camps of the army. What nature requires is close by and easy to obtain. All that sweat is for superfluities. We wear out our fine clothes, grow old in army tents, hurl ourselves against foreign shores, and for what? Everything we need is already at hand. Anyone who is on good terms with poverty is rich.

Seneca, Letters. 14.18

He who feels the need of wealth also fears for his wealth. But no one has enjoyment from so vexed a good. He is eager to add to it; and while he is thinking about its increase, he is forgetting about its use. He is collecting on his accounts- pounding the pavement of the forum- flipping through his ledger. He is not master but factotum.

Seneca, Letters. 15.11

Dismiss at last those treacherous goods that are more valuable in expectation than they are in attainment. If there were anything solid in them, we would eventually be sated with them; as it is, they make us thirsty even as we drink.

Seneca, Letters. 32.5

My wish is this: may you be your own master; may your mind, which is now driven this way and that by its concerns, come at last to a halt, sure and content in itself; may you come to understand those true goods that belong to you in the moment you understand them, and so feel no need of additional years. In order to rise above necessities, to gain one's discharge, to be free, one must live a life that is already complete.

Seneca, Letters. 44.7

What, then, is the mistake people make, seeing that everyone wants a happy life? They take the instruments used by happiness to be happiness itself, and so abandon the very thing they are seeking. For the chief point in a happy life is to be solidly secure and unshakably confident of that state; and yet they gather up the causes of anxiety and haul, no, drag those burdens behind them on life's treacherous journey. For that reason they recede further and further from what they seek to attain, and the greater their efforts, the greater the hinderance they create for themselves. It is like hurrying in a maze: their very haste impedes them.

Seneca, Letters. 45.9

...the happy person is not the one ordinary people call happy, not the one who has been showered with money, but rather the one whose every good resides in the mind. That one is upright and exalted; he spurns underfoot the objects of wonder; he would not trade his life for any other that he sees.

Seneca, Letters. 61.4

Our life is well enough equipped. Yet we are greedy for life's equipment. We think we are missing something, and we always will think that. To have enough of life: neither days nor years can give us that, but only the mind.

Seneca, Letters. 74.10-11

The person who is determined to be happy should make up his mind that the one good thing is honorable conduct. For if he imagines that there is any other good, first of all he thinks ill of providence, since many uncomfortable things happen to just men, and since whatever gifts we do receive are small and of brief duration compared with the age of the universe. It is in consequence of this complaint that we are such thankless interpreters of the divine. We complain that our blessings are not ours forever, and that they are few, unreliable, and fleeting.

Seneca, Letters. 81.28

As long as we are seeking a benefit, there is nothing we value more highly; once we have obtained it, there is nothing we value less. What makes us forget the favors we have obtained? Our desire is to obtain more: we don't think about what we have been granted already but only about our next request. We are drawn from what is right by wealth, honor, power, and everything else that is precious in our eyes, though cheap in actual worth.

Seneca, Letters. 119.6

Would you rather have a large amount, or enough? Those who have a large amount want more, which is proof that they do not yet have enough. The one who has enough has attained the one thing the rich can never get: a stopping point.

Epictetus, Handbook. 33,7

In things relating to the body, such as food, drink, clothing, housing, and household staff, limit yourself to what satisfies your basic needs, and cut out everything that's pretentious or self-indulgent.

Epictetus, Discourses. 3.9.15-16

"But if I make judgements my primary concern, I'll be just like you, with no land to my name, no silver goblets, no fine livestock."
"I think all I need to say in response to this is that I don't need these things. As for you, however, the more you have, the more you'll need, so that, willy-nilly, you'll be poorer than I am."

Epictetus, Discourses. 3.9.21-22

All your possessions seem small to you, but all mine seem great to me. Your desire is unfulfilled, mine has already been fulfilled. When a child puts his hand inside a narrow-necked jar and tries to extract some tidbits, what happens? If he fills his hand, he can't get them out, and then he starts to cry. Let a few of them go and you'll get the rest out. The same goes for you too: let your desire go. If you don't want many things, you'll get what you want.

Epictetus Discourses. 4.3.9-12

For I am free and a friend of God, so that I willingly obey him. I shouldn't lay claim to anything else, neither body, nor possessions, nor political power, nor status- in a word, nothing. Because he doesn't want me to lay claim to them. After all, if he did want that, he'd have made them good for me. But, as things are, he didn't do that, and that's why it's impossible for me to disobey his commands.

Protect your good always, and as for everything else, be content with what's been allotted to you, as long as you make rational use of it, and don't ask for anything more. Otherwise, you'll be miserable and wretched, impeded and obstructed. These are the laws that have been relayed to us from above; these are God's commandments.

Epictetus, Fragments. 2

Anyone who's dissatisfied with the circumstances assigned to him by fortune is unskilled in the art of living, while anyone who nobly endures his circumstances and makes reasonable use of what they have to offer deserves to be called a good person.

If someone is discontent with their current circumstances, and is always looking forward to something more, they have already disposed themselves towards discontentment; and even if circumstances improve, they are likely to maintain their disposition of discontent, and continue to look forward to yet more improvements.

If someone is content with their current circumstance, and thankful for what they already have; when circumstances change, they can maintain their course of a content disposition, even if there is not a significant improvement in their circumstance.

If you feel that you need something external to complete you, you will not feel complete even when externals change. You have already disposed yourself towards the idea that you are discontent and wanting for more externals. A change of circumstance does not bring about a change in disposition, but the disposition will adapt and continue to seek for yet more externals. If your focus is on externals, you do not better your person when obtaining more things, but your person is debilitated with the reinforcement of a habitual misdirect.

Happiness is not about controlling your external circumstances, but about finding peace within. What if you were content within, regardless of your current circumstances? Even if your circumstances change, you are still a person who is content. When you become indifferent to externals, you are actually better prepared to receive an increase; as you are not as emotionally vested in the outcome, and can better adapt to the ever-changing circumstances of life with a healthy sense of detachment.

God is more interested in improving your person than in improving your circumstances.

On Single-Minded Focus

Jesus warned against the evil eye, which signifies envy. Attention to the things of God requires a single-minded focus, which cannot be shared with greed for mammon, which is worldly riches.

Matthew 6:22-24

The light of the body is the eye: if therefore thine eye be single, thy whole body shall be full of light. 23 But if thine eye be evil, thy whole body shall be full of darkness. If therefore the light that is in thee be darkness, how great is that darkness! 24 No man can serve two masters: for either he will hate the one, and love the other; or else he will hold to the one, and despise the other. Ye cannot serve God and mammon.

Luke 10:41-42

And Jesus answered and said unto her, Martha, Martha, thou art careful and troubled about many things: 42 But one thing is needful: and Mary hath chosen that good part, which shall not be taken away from her.

Seneca, Letters. 45.12-13

Show us that much time is wasted pursuing what is superfluous, that many people miss out on life by going after life's equipment. Observe individuals, and study people in general, and you will find every one of us living for tomorrow.

"Is there any harm in that?" you say. Yes, endless harm. For they are not living; they are only about to live. Everything is deferred. Even if we were paying attention- life would slip by us; as it is, we put off living, and our lives race past us as if they belonged to someone else- ending on the last day, yet lost to us every day.

Seneca, Letters. 53.9
Get rid of everything that stands in your way; make time for excellence of mind. No one gets there while occupied with business.

Seneca, Letters. 59.14
Joy is your aim, but you are off course: you think that you will get there amid riches and accolades; in other words, you seek joy in the midst of anxiety! You go after those things on grounds that they will bestow happiness and pleasure, but in reality they are causes of pain.

Epictetus, Handbook. 13
For it's not easy, believe me, to keep your will in compliance with nature and also to secure external things for yourself. If you care about the one, you're bound to neglect the other.

Epictetus, Discourses. 4.6.25
"But other people will be better off than me and will be promoted over me."
"But that makes perfect sense, doesn't it? If people have been intent on something, they're bound to have the advantage in it, the thing they've worked at, aren't they? They've been intent on obtaining political power, while you've been intent on judgements. They've been intent on becoming rich, you on how to use your impressions."

Epictetus, Discourses. 4.9.1-3

Whenever you see someone in a position of political power, set against it the fact that you have no need of political power. Whenever you see someone making a fortune, see what you have instead of that.

If you have nothing to put in its place, you see, you feel sorry for yourself, but if you have no need of wealth, you should realize that what you have is more than what he has and far more valuable. One man longs for a beautiful wife; you have your not longing for a beautiful wife. Does that strike you as insignificant? Yet how much would these very people give- the rich, the powerful, the men with beautiful wives- to be able to regard wealth as unimportant, and political power, and even these wives of theirs whom they love and gain?

Epictetus, Discourses. 4.10.25

It's impossible for you to take care that you have externals and to take care of your command center. If you want the former, forget about the latter. Otherwise, you'll have neither one nor the other, because you'll be pulled in two directions. So if you want the latter, you must give up the former.

Aurelius, Meditations. 3.6

Nothing will sooner prevent your true spirit from flourishing or be more difficult to root out than the distraction of a divided loyalty. Nothing whatsoever- neither popularity, nor wealth, nor power, nor the pleasures of the flesh, nor anything of the sort- should compete in your affection for the good that flows from reason and neighborliness. Although for a while these inferior loves may seem quite compatible with an orderly life, they will soon overpower and destroy you. Simply and freely choose what is best, and never let go of it.

Aurelius, Meditations. 6.16
Attend to this [the voice of reason], and nothing else will matter. But what if you continue to hanker after other things as well? Then don't expect to be free or fulfilled or content. Instead you will be haunted by fear and envy- suspicious of those who might rob you of what you have and scheming against those who have what you want.

Aurelius, Meditations. 7.3
Bear in mind that the measure of a man is the worth of the things he cares about.

The storms of life will try to blow us off course, but the wise man will remain steadfast and immovable in his direction of purpose.

Ephesians 4:14
That we henceforth be no more children, tossed to and fro, and carried about with every wind of doctrine, by the sleight of men, and cunning craftiness, whereby they lie in wait to deceive;

James 1:5-8
If any of you lack wisdom, let him ask of God, that giveth to all men liberally, and upbraideth not; and it shall be given him. 6 But let him ask in faith, nothing wavering. For he that wavereth is like a wave of the sea driven with the wind and tossed. 7 For let not that man think that he shall receive any thing of the Lord. 8 A double minded man is unstable in all his ways.

Seneca, Letters. 35.4

If you ever want to find out whether anything has been achieved, observe whether your intentions are the same today as they were yesterday. A change of intention shows that the mind is at sea, drifting here and there as carried by the wind. A thing that is well grounded does not move about. That is how it is for the completely wise person, and also to some extent for the one who is making progress towards wisdom. What is the difference, then? The progressor moves, but does not shift position; he merely bobs in place. The wise person does not move at all.

On the Desire for Worldly Advantage

Doesn't everyone want what is good for themselves? What's wrong with that? Nothing, as long as you properly understand what is "good". Is it *good* to have power and riches, and to fulfill the desires of the body at will? Is it not rather *good* to have the peace of mind which flows from the virtues of wisdom? The desire for externals comes with a cost of internal tranquility, and as such, is not a *good* thing.

> James 4:1-3
> From whence come wars and fightings among you? come they not hence, even of your lusts that war in your members? 2 Ye lust, and have not: ye kill, and desire to have, and cannot obtain: ye fight and war, yet ye have not, because ye ask not. 3 Ye ask, and receive not, because ye ask amiss, that ye may consume it upon your lusts.

> Seneca, Letters. 123.13
> We shall be able to reach that point if we understand that there are two kinds of things that can either entice or repel us. The enticing ones are wealth, pleasures, beauty, ambition, and everything else that is seductive and pleasing. We are repelled by hard physical work, death, pain, public disapproval, and an austere diet. Hence we should train ourselves neither to fear that latter things nor to desire the former. We should contend against our inclinations, resisting the attractive things and advancing against those that assail us.

Epictetus, Discourses. 1.22.14

If it's good for me to have a plot of land, it's also good for me to take my neighbor's plot of land. If it's good for me to have a toga, it's also good for me to steal one from the bathhouse. This is how war starts, and civil strife, tyranny, intrigue.

Epictetus, Discourses. 1.27.10-12

The point is that the root cause of passion is wanting something and not getting it. That's why, if I'm able to alter my external circumstances to suit my wishes, I do so, and if I can't, I'm ready to gouge out the eyes of the person who's obstructing me. It's because it's human nature to find it unbearable to be deprived of something good or to experience something bad.

Epictetus, Discourses. 3.2.3

The most important and urgent of these domains is the one that has to do with the passions. A passion is only ever the result of frustrated desire or ineffective aversion. This is the domain that entails mental turmoil, confusion, wretchedness, misery, sorrow, grief, and fear, and which makes us envious and jealous, until we can't even listen to reason.

Aurelius, Meditations. 3,6

"But the best is whatever works to my advantage," you say. Then study your advantage carefully. If it's to the advantage of your reasonable self, seize hold of it. If it's merely to the advantage of your animal self, admit it and don't try to pretend it's more than that. Only be sure of your judgment.

We seek to obtain the maximum degree of worldly advantage at the minimal amount of painful labor, and regard it as unfair if someone gets something for nothing; yet even if the things of this world were to come to us for free, they are never without a cost, for they inevitably cost us in the very acquisition of them. Even if someone were to get away with a crime, they suffer in the instant from the loss of character which results in the deed itself. Such apparent advantages should never be envied.

Mark 8:36-37
For what shall it profit a man, if he shall gain the whole world, and lose his own soul? 37 Or what shall a man give in exchange for his soul?

Romans 1:27b
...and receiving in themselves that recompence of their error which was meet.

Seneca, Letters. 42.6-7
Those things we compete for- the things to which we devote so much effort- offer us either no advantage, or greater disadvantage. Some are superfluities; others are not worth the trouble, but we don't realize it. We think things come for free, when in fact their price is very steep. Here is what makes our idiocy quite plain: we think the only things we pay for are those are those we spend our money on. The things we call free are those on which we spend our very selves. Things we wouldn't be willing to pay for if it meant giving up our house for them, or some pleasant or productive estate, we are quite ready to obtain at the cost of anxiety, of danger, of losing our freedom, our decency, our time. You see, we treat ourselves as if we were more worthless than anything else.

Seneca, Letters. 87.25

Yet the greatest penalty for criminal acts is in the acts themselves. You are mistaken if you make them wait for the prison or the executioner: such acts are punished right away when performed, indeed in the very act of performing them.

Seneca, Letters. 97.14

Because the first and greatest punishment for wrongdoers is the fact of having done wrong. No crime, even one embellished with the gifts of fortune or protected and safeguarded thereby, is free from punishment, since the penalty for crime lies in the crime.

Seneca, Letters. 115.16

For greed never goes unpunished. Yet greed in itself is punishment enough. What tears, what pain it costs us! How it suffers over what it lacks- and how it suffers over what it has acquired! There are the day-to-day worries too: the more a person has, the more anxiety he feels. Money is even more of a torment to those who have it than to those who are trying to get it. How they lament each loss! For they lose large sums, and think them even larger than they are. Even if fortune takes nothing away from them, whatever they fail to acquire seems like a loss.

Aurelius, Meditations. 9.4

The sinner sins against himself. The unjust man does injustice to himself by making himself bad.

Aurelius, Meditations. 9.20

Another's wrongdoing– leave it alone.

On Submission to the Will of God

Rather than living a life of struggle to subject the external circumstances of this world to the power of our will; we can trust that all things are under the control of the good and wise discretion of divine providence, and so find peace with an acceptance of whatever happens as being properly ordained for us. Jesus lived in perfect submission to the Father, even when that ultimately resulted in his own painful death.

Matthew 6:10
Thy kingdom come. Thy will be done in earth, as it is in heaven.

John 5:19
Then answered Jesus and said unto them, Verily, verily, I say unto you, The Son can do nothing of himself, but what he seeth the Father do: for what things soever he doeth, these also doeth the Son likewise.

Luke 22:42b
... nevertheless not my will, but thine, be done.

Seneca, Letters. 107.9
No matter what happens, we should think that it had to happen and not wish to reproach nature. It is best to endure what you cannot correct, and to go along uncomplainingly with the divinity who is in charge of the entire course of events. It is a poor soldier who groans as he follows his commander.

Seneca, Letters. 120.12

The perfect man, the one in possession of virtue, never cursed his luck and never reacted to circumstances with a grim face. Believing himself to be a citizen and soldier of the world, he took on each labor as though it were a command. He treated no incident as an annoying nuisance and misfortune but as a task assigned to himself. "Whatever it is," he says, "this is mine to do. It is rough and tough, so let's get busy!" Hence there was no mistaking the evident greatness of the man who never groaned about troubles and never complained about his fate. He gave many people an understanding of himself. He shone like a light in the dark, drawing attention to himself, because he was calm and gentle, equally resigned to human affairs and to acts of God.

Epictetus, Handbook. 1.1
Some things are up to us and some are not.

Epictetus, Discourses. 4.1.89-90
I've never been prevented from doing what I want, nor have I been forced to do what I don't want. Both are impossible, because I've submitted my inclinations to God. He wants me to have a fever; that's what I want too. He wants me to have an inclination for something; that's what I want too. He wants me to desire; that's what I want too. He wants me to get something; that's what I want too. Unless he wants something, I don't want it. And so I'm willing to die or be tortured. Under these circumstances, who can impede or constrain me contrary to my own judgment? No one, any more that he could impede or constrain Zeus.

Epictetus, Discourses. 4.1.101-102
So why would I fight God? Why would I want things that aren't subject to my wishes, things that weren't unconditionally given to

me? How do I possess them? As conditionally as they were given and for as long as they're available to me. But the giver can take them away again. So what would be the point of resistance? Not to mention how stupid it would be of me to try to use force against one who is stronger than me- and, more importantly, how wrong it would be. After all, how did I come to have these things when I came into the world? They were gifts from my father. And who gave them to him? Who made the sun, the fruits of the earth, the seasons? Who made human society and community?

Epictetus, Discourses. 4.1.172
For the sake of true freedom, which is immune to intrigue and safe from harm, won't you give up what God has given you when he asks for it back? Won't you prepare yourself by training not just, as Plato says, for death, but for being tortured, exiled, and whipped? In short, won't you train yourself to give back things that aren't yours?

Aurelius, Meditations. 10.5
Whatever happens to you was destined to happen from before time began. Your entire existence as well as the smallest details of your works and days were woven into the woof of cause, the weft of effect from all eternity.

Aurelius, Meditations. 10.20
What nature gives is best, and best too at the time it is given.

Aurelius, Meditations. 10.25

The slave who flees his master is a runaway. The law too is a master, and whoever breaks it is in the same position as the runaway slave. Likewise, those who become irritable, angry, or afraid because something has already happened, is just happening, or is about to happen are, in effect, refusing to accept the natural and causal laws of the universe. In giving way to irritation, anger, or fear, they are no better than runaway slaves.

On Facing Challenges

When we are faced with hardships, we should welcome them with determination, as an athlete-in-training who tackles increasing challenges with ambition. Difficulties do not come to us through random happenstance, but they are ordained for us to make us stronger.

1 Corinthians 9:24-27
Know ye not that they which run in a race run all, but one receiveth the prize? So run, that ye may obtain. 25 And every man that striveth for the mastery is temperate in all things. Now they do it to obtain a corruptible crown; but we an incorruptible. 26 I therefore so run, not as uncertainly; so fight I, not as one that beateth the air: 27 But I keep under my body, and bring it into subjection: lest that by any means, when I have preached to others, I myself should be a castaway.

2 Timothy 4:6-8
For I am now ready to be offered, and the time of my departure is at hand. 7 I have fought a good fight, I have finished my course, I have kept the faith: 8 Henceforth there is laid up for me a crown of righteousness, which the Lord, the righteous judge, shall give me at that day: and not to me only, but unto all them also that love his appearing.

Seneca, Letters. 12.9
Glad and cheerful, let us say, as we go to our rest, "I have done living; I have run the race that fortune set for me."

Seneca, Letters. 67.14

To lie in undisturbed calm, with nothing to rouse yourself toward, nothing to strive after, nothing to denounce or contend against, testing the firmness of your mind: that is not tranquility; it is enfeeblement.

Epictetus, Handbook. 51.2

And, in the event that you're faced with something painful or pleasant, or something that will enhance or damage your reputation, remember that the contest is on- that here, now, are the Olympic Games, that procrastination is no longer an option, and that just one defeat and and surrender determines whether your progress is ruined or remains intact.

Epictetus, Discourses. 1.24:1-2a

"A person's caliber is revealed by difficult circumstances, and so, when a difficulty occurs, think of it as God pitting you, as a trainer might, against a tough training partner."
"To what end?" someone asked.
"To help you become an Olympic victor, which takes sweat."

Aurelius, Meditations. 4.2

Never act without purpose and resolve, or without the means to finish the job.

Aurelius, Meditations. 10.3

But remember, you have the power within you to endure anything, for your mere opinion can render it tolerable, perhaps even acceptable, by regarding it as an opportunity for enlightenment or a matter of duty.

Aurelius, Meditations. 10.31

Persevere, then, until you have learned everything life has to teach you, the way a healthy stomach digests all sorts of food and a roaring fire converts whatever is heaped on it to heat and light.

Aurelius, Meditations. 10.33

Whenever anything is hindered, its condition deteriorates and becomes worse, whereas a man actually becomes better and more praiseworthy when he overcomes what hinders him through the use of reason.

On The Fear of Death

The powers of this world enslave others through fear– ultimately the fear of death. If you can overcome the fear of death, then you can overcome fear altogether, and these powers lose their hold over your mind.

Luke 12:4

And I say unto you my friends, Be not afraid of them that kill the body, and after that have no more that they can do.

Hebrews 2:14-15

Forasmuch then as the children are partakers of flesh and blood, he also himself likewise took part of the same; that through death he might destroy him that had the power of death, that is, the devil; 15 And deliver them who through fear of death were all their lifetime subject to bondage.

Seneca, Letters. 74.3

But of all the suffering crowds of humankind, the greatest is of those who are troubled by the thought of death. That thought meets them at every turn, for death may come from any direction. Like troops passing through enemy territory, they must be looking around all the time, turning their heads at every sound. Unless this fear is driven from the breast, we live with quaking hearts.

Epictetus, Discourses. 1.29.5-7

So suppose a tyrant threatens me and summons me to his presence. 'What am I threatened with?' I ask. If he says, 'I'll clap you in irons,' I say, 'He's threatening my hands and feet.' If he says, 'I'll cut off your head,' I say, 'He's threatening my neck.' If he says, 'I'll throw you in prison,' I say, 'Now it's my whole body.' And I give the same response if he threatens me with banishment.

"So he doesn't actually threaten you at all?"

"Yes, that's right, as long as I feel that these things are nothing to me. But if any of those prospects makes me afraid, then he threatens me."

Epictetus, Discourses. 1.30.1

If you're ever in the presence of a powerful man, remember that someone else is looking down from on high at what's going on, and that it's him you have to please rather than that man.

Epictetus, Discourses. 3.7.35

'Do this and don't do that, or I shall throw you into prison.' This isn't the way to govern rational creatures. No: 'Do as Zeus has ordained, otherwise you'll be damaged and harmed.' What kind of harm? Not acting as you should-- that kind of harm. You'll destroy the trustworthy person in you, the self-respecting person, the modest person. There's no point in looking for any greater damage than that.

Epictetus, Discourses. 3.26.38-39

Can't you see that this thing, the source of all human troubles and debasement and cowardice, isn't death, but rather the fear of death? That is what you must train yourself to cope with, that is where all your reasoning should tend, and your exercises and your reading. Then you'll appreciate that this is the only way in which people can be free.

Epictetus, Discourses. 4.7.4-6

Imagine someone, then, who's completely indifferent about whether he lives or dies, and willingly accepts his lot: when he comes into a tyrant's presence, what's to stop him from doing so without fear?

Nothing.

Now imagine someone who feels the same way about his possessions, children, and wife as that man feels about his body. Imagine he's so crazy and witless that he doesn't care whether or not he has these things. Think of a child playing with shards of pottery, who tries to win the game, but doesn't care about the shards. Like this child, our man has come to consider material things unimportant, but enjoys playing and occupying himself with them. Under these circumstances, is there any tyrant or are there any guards with their swords who could make him afraid?

On Facing Death

When it comes to actually facing death, this is the ultimate test. Even if one is not threatened with an imminent death, it is a helpful mental exercise to contemplate your own mortality (Latin: "Memento Mori"), and to use it as a measure against the transitory concerns of this life. Christianity embodies a similar death-focused theme with the perpetual remembrance of the death of Christ, a ritual instituted by Christ himself.

> 1 Corinthians 11:23-26
> For I have received of the Lord that which also I delivered unto you, That the Lord Jesus the same night in which he was betrayed took bread: 24 And when he had given thanks, he brake it, and said, Take, eat: this is my body, which is broken for you: this do in remembrance of me. 25 After the same manner also he took the cup, when he had supped, saying, This cup is the new testament in my blood: this do ye, as oft as ye drink it, in remembrance of me. 26 For as often as ye eat this bread, and drink this cup, ye do shew the Lord's death till he come.

> 2 Corinthians 4:10-11
> 10 Always bearing about in the body the dying of the Lord Jesus, that the life also of Jesus might be made manifest in our body. 11 For we which live are alway delivered unto death for Jesus' sake, that the life also of Jesus might be made manifest in our mortal flesh.

> Seneca, Letters. 26.5

Death will disclose to me what progress I have made. Thus I am unafraid as I prepare myself for that day when the artifices and disguises will be stripped away and I shall make judgment of myself.

Seneca, Letters. 26.10
There is but one chain that binds us: the love of life. That, admittedly, we may not discard; yet we must lessen it, lest anything detain us when commanded by our situation, or hinder us from readiness to do at once what must be done someday.

Upon dying, we must let go of everything we have in this world. If we can face death early through our own conscious awareness, we can experience a sort of death to self; and by this we are able to detach ourselves from avarice, ambition, lust, and the desires of this world. As we make our peace with the prospect of death, we attain a more spiritual life.

Seneca, Letters. 92.31,32
Getting to the heavens would be a mighty task, were it not that the mind is returning whence it came. Once it has found the way, it travels boldly, disdainful of everything else, heedless of money or gold or silver, which fully deserve the darkness in which they have lain. It estimates their value not by the gleam that dazzles the eyes of the ignorant, but by the dross from which our cupidity has unearthed and separated them. That is to say, the elevated spirit knows that genuine riches are found elsewhere than the treasure trove, and that what ought to be fully stocked is not one's money chest but oneself.
The mind is entitled to be master over everything, to be granted ownership of the world, to have its property extend from east to west, and like the gods to possess all things. From its high seat, it

looks down on the wealthy amid their resources, all of them less happy with what they own than they are saddened by what belongs to others.

Seneca, Letters. 98.10
Yet people are so flawed and so heedless of the destination to which the passage of each day is pushing them that they are caught by surprise when they lose something, even though on a single day they will lose everything. Those things you are considered to own are in your home, but they are not yours. Nothing is secure for the insecure, nothing is lasting and invincible for a person who is fragile. It is not only our property that has to go: it is ourselves too; and this very fact, if only we understand it, is consoling. Be calm when something goes: you must go as well.

Seneca, Letters. 99.31
To the person who is weeping and longing for one who was snatched away in youth, let's say this as well: young or old, every life is equally short when compared with that of the universe. For any possible lifespan is less even that what one would call a tiny bit. A tiny bit is at least something, but this life of ours is practically nothing.

Seneca, Letters. 114.27
But nothing will do as much to help you toward self-control in all things as the reflection that life is short, and the little we have of it is uncertain. In every act, keep your eyes on death.

Seneca, Letters. 120.17-18

Nothing is enough for us, soon to die though we are. Indeed, we are already dying. Every day we stand closer to our last, and every hour thrusts us towards the place where we are bound to fall. See what blindness affects our minds. What I call the future is happening right now, and a large part of it is already past. For the time we have lived is already where it was before we were alive. We are wrong to fear our last day: each day contributes the same amount to death. The faltering footstep does not weary us; it only shows that we are weary. Our last day arrives at death, but every one of our days approaches it. Death does not grab us, it picks away at us.

On the Fruition of Wisdom

Wisdom cannot be gained as easily as knowledge, as if it were merely information to be grasped. It must be gained through experience and lived out. This takes time, just as it takes time for plants to grow.

> Mark 4:26-29
> And he said, So is the kingdom of God, as if a man should cast seed into the ground; 27 And should sleep, and rise night and day, and the seed should spring and grow up, he knoweth not how. 28 For the earth bringeth forth fruit of herself; first the blade, then the ear, after that the full corn in the ear. 29 But when the fruit is brought forth, immediately he putteth in the sickle, because the harvest is come.

> Epictetus, Discourses. 1.15:7-8
> "Anything of importance takes time," said Epictetus, "even a bunch of grapes or a fig. If what you were telling me now was 'I want a fig,' I'd reply, 'Be patient. First let the tree flower and then fruit, and then wait for the fruit to ripen.' So given that it takes time for even a fig tree's fruit to mature, and it doesn't happen overnight, are you wanting to get the fruit of human intelligence so quickly and easily? You shouldn't expect that, even if I were to promise you it myself."

The words of the wise are like small seeds– if they are taken to heart, they can bring about a significant transformation of life.

Mark 4:30-32

And he said, Whereunto shall we liken the kingdom of God? or with what comparison shall we compare it? 31 It is like a grain of mustard seed, which, when it is sown in the earth, is less than all the seeds that be in the earth: 32 But when it is sown, it groweth up, and becometh greater than all herbs, and shooteth out great branches; so that the fowls of the air may lodge under the shadow of it.

Seneca, Letters. 38.2

They should be scattered like seeds. A seed is just a little thing, and yet when it lands in the right spot, it unfolds its resources and expands into a great and growing plant. Reasoning does the same: when you examine it, it is of small extent; but when you put it into effect, it grows. Only a few words are said, but if the mind receives them well, they become tall and strong.

Different kinds of people respond differently to the same teaching. It takes a person of quality to nurture wisdom to proper maturity.

Matthew 13:18-23

Hear ye therefore the parable of the sower. 19 When any one heareth the word of the kingdom, and understandeth it not, then cometh the wicked one, and catcheth away that which was sown in his heart. This is he which received seed by the way side. 20 But he that received the seed into stony places, the same is he that heareth the word, and anon with joy receiveth it; 21 Yet hath he not root in himself, but dureth for a while: for when tribulation or persecution ariseth because of the word, by and by he is offended. 22 He also that received seed among the thorns is he that heareth the word; and the care of this world, and the deceitfulness of riches, choke the word, and he becometh unfruitful. 23 But he that received seed into the good ground is he that heareth the word, and understandeth it; which also beareth fruit, and bringeth forth, some an hundredfold, some sixty, some thirty.

Epictetus, Discourses. 4.8.37
That's the kind of plant you are too. You've flowered before your time, and winter will wither you. Remember what farmers say about their seeds when an unseasonably early warm spell occurs. They worry that the seeds will shoot up and then a single frost will grip them and expose their weakness. You too need to be careful, man. You've shot up and rushed to gain a reputation before your time.

A plant does not bear fruit for its own benefit, but for the benefit of others. Ripe fruit contains the seeds for future life.

John 12:24-25
Verily, verily, I say unto you, Except a corn of wheat fall into the ground and die, it abideth alone: but if it die, it bringeth forth much fruit. 25 He that loveth his life shall lose it; and he that hateth his life in this world shall keep it unto life eternal.

Epictetus, Discourses. 2.6.11-14
I mean, look, why do ears of wheat grow? It's so that they can become dry, isn't it? And they become dry so that they can be harvested, don't they? Because they don't exist in isolation. So if they were conscious, they'd be bound to pray never to be harvested, wouldn't they? But it's a curse for ears of wheat not to be harvested. By the same token, I assure you, it's a curse for people

not to die; it's no different from wheat nor ripening and not being harvested. But since it is we ourselves who are bound to be harvested, and we also understand that we are the things being harvested, we get upset.

The proper fruition of wisdom occurs in its own way and time, and cannot be brought about by force of will.

John 15:5
I am the vine, ye are the branches: He that abideth in me, and I in him, the same bringeth forth much fruit: for without me ye can do nothing.

Aurelius, Meditations. 5.6
There are three kinds of men in this world. The first, when he helps someone out, makes it known that he expects something in return. The second would never be so bold, but in his mind he knows what he has done and considers the other person to be in his debt. The third somehow doesn't realize what he has done, but he's like a vine that bears its fruit, and asks for nothing more than the pleasure of producing grapes. A horse gallops, a dog hunts, a bee makes honey, one man helps another, and the vine bears fruit in due season.

Aurelius, Meditations. 9.10
Everything bears fruit- Man, God, the Universe- each in its own season. It doesn't matter that this manner of speaking is customarily reserved for the vine and other plants. Reason also bears fruit, both for itself and for everything else, and all its fruit tastes of sweet reasonableness.

On Loving Others

When we recognize the divine in ourselves and others, the natural consequence is that we should love others as we love ourselves.

Luke 6:31
And as ye would that men should do to you, do ye also to them likewise.

1 John 3:1-3
Behold, what manner of love the Father hath bestowed upon us, that we should be called the sons of God: therefore the world knoweth us not, because it knew him not. 2 Beloved, now are we the sons of God, and it doth not yet appear what we shall be: but we know that, when he shall appear, we shall be like him; for we shall see him as he is. 3 And every man that hath this hope in him purifieth himself, even as he is pure.

1 John 4:20-21
If a man say, I love God, and hateth his brother, he is a liar: for he that loveth not his brother whom he hath seen, how can he love God whom he hath not seen? 21 And this commandment have we from him, That he who loveth God love his brother also.

Acts 17:28
For in him we live, and move, and have our being; as certain also of your own poets have said, For we are also his offspring.

Aratus, Phaenomena. 1,

https://www.theoi.com/Text/AratusPhaenomena.html
For we are also his offspring; and he in his kindness unto men giveth favourable signs and wakeneth the people to work, reminding them of livelihood

Cleanthes, Hymn to Zeus. 1:1,2
https://www.elfinspell.com/ClassicalTexts/Rolleston-Epictetus/Te
achingsOfEpictetus-HymnToZeus.html
For we are Thy offspring, taking the image only of Thy voice, as many mortal things as live and move upon the earth.

Epictetus, Discourses. 1.3.1-2

If one could fully and properly assimilate the idea that we're all principally children of God- that God is the father of both human beings and gods- I doubt he would ever think of himself as base or despicable. If Caesar were to adopt you, you'd be insufferably arrogant, so how could it fail to be a source of pride if you knew you were a son of God?

Aurelius, Meditations. 4.12

Arm yourself for action with these two thoughts: first, do only what your sovereign and lawgiving reason tells you is for the good of others; and second, do not hesitate to change course if someone is able to show you where you are mistaken or point out a better way.

Aurelius, Meditations. 6.39

Live in harmony with everything around you, and love- without reservations or conditions- those with whom you live and work.

While the natural man seeks his own advantage, even at the expense of others; the enlightened soul understands that it is better to give than to receive.

Acts 20:35
I have shewed you all things, how that so labouring ye ought to support the weak, and to remember the words of the Lord Jesus, how he said, It is more blessed to give than to receive.

Seneca, Letters. 81.10
The wise person will take stock in his mind of how much he has received and from whom, and when, where, why, and how. That's why we say that only the sage knows how to render thanks, just as only he knows how to confer a benefit. Naturally, this is the same wise person who finds more joy in giving than others do in receiving.

Rufus, Lectures. 6.6-7
...when hardship comes we think an evil has come upon us, and when pleasure comes our way we think that a good has befallen us; we dread death as the most extreme misfortune; we cling to life as the greatest blessing, and when we give away money we grieve as if we were injured, but upon receiving it we rejoice as if a benefit had been conferred. Similarly with the majority of other things, we do not meet circumstances in accordance with right principles, but rather we follow wretched habit. Since, then, I repeat, all this is the case, the person who is in training must strive to habituate himself not to love pleasure, not to avoid hardship, not to be infatuated with living, not to fear death, and in the case of goods or money not to place receiving above giving.

Aurelius, Meditations. 9.1

He sins who acts unjustly. All rational creatures, by nature's deep design and purpose, are created for one another. They are meant to help those who deserve help and in no way to harm one another.

Giving to others has value as an expression of love, and not merely for the utilitarian value of the gift.

Luke 21:1-4

And he looked up, and saw the rich men casting their gifts into the treasury. 2 And he saw also a certain poor widow casting in thither two mites. 3 And he said, Of a truth I say unto you, that this poor widow hath cast in more than they all: 4 For all these have of their abundance cast in unto the offerings of God: but she of her penury hath cast in all the living that she had.

2 Corinthians 9:7

Every man according as he purposeth in his heart, so let him give; not grudgingly, or of necessity: for God loveth a cheerful giver.

Seneca, Letters. 81.6

Every benefit merits gratitude matching the attitude of the giver: one weighs not the size of the benefit, but the willingness to bestow it.

On Purity

If we realize that we are in God, and God is in us, we should be conscious not to defile the body with sexual perversion.

1 Corinthians 3:16-17
Know ye not that ye are the temple of God, and that the Spirit of God dwelleth in you? 17 If any man defile the temple of God, him shall God destroy; for the temple of God is holy, which temple ye are.

1 Corinthians 6:15
Know ye not that your bodies are the members of Christ? shall I then take the members of Christ, and make them the members of an harlot? God forbid.

Rufus, Lectures. 12,3
But of all sexual relations those involving adultery are most unlawful, and no more tolerable are those of men with men, because it is monstrous thing and contrary to nature.

Epictetus, Discourses. 2.8.11-13
But you are a leader and a fragment of God. You have, within yourself, a bit of him. So why are you ignorant of your relationship with him? Why don't you know where you've come from? Shouldn't you remember, when you eat, who is eating and being nourished, and when you have sex, who is having sex? When you're in company, when you take exercise, when you make conversation, don't you recognize that you're feeding God, exercising God? You

carry God around, and yet, poor fool that you are, you don't know it. Do you take me to be talking about some external god made of silver or gold? You carry him around within yourself, and you fail to realize that you defile him with impure thoughts and unclean acts.

Epictetus, Handbook. 33.8
As for sex, keep yourself as chaste as possible before marriage, and if you do engage in it, keep it within conventional bounds.

Those who focus on externals are often more concerned about what they eat than what they think about or who they sleep with. The wise man carefully guards his internal self from impurity.

Matthew 15:11
Not that which goeth into the mouth defileth a man; but that which cometh out of the mouth, this defileth a man.

Matthew 15:17-20
Do not ye yet understand, that whatsoever entereth in at the mouth goeth into the belly, and is cast out into the draught? 18 But those things which proceed out of the mouth come forth from the heart; and they defile the man. 19 For out of the heart proceed evil thoughts, murders, adulteries, fornications, thefts, false witness, blasphemies: 20 These are the things which defile a man: but to eat with unwashen hands defileth not a man.

Epictetus, Handbook. 48

The position and character of a non-philosopher: never expect benefit or harm to come from oneself, but only from the outside world. The position and character of a philosopher: only expect benefit and harm to come from oneself

On Friendship

A wise man is known by the company he keeps. One should exercise discretion in making friends and spending time with others. Rather than trying to please the crowd, the wise man knows when to simply walk away.

1 Corinthians 15:33
Be not deceived: evil communications corrupt good manners.

1 Peter 4:3-4
For the time past of our life may suffice us to have wrought the will of the Gentiles, when we walked in lasciviousness, lusts, excess of wine, revellings, banquetings, and abominable idolatries: 4 Wherein they think it strange that ye run not with them to the same excess of riot, speaking evil of you:

James 4:4
Ye adulterers and adulteresses, know ye not that the friendship of the world is enmity with God? whosoever therefore will be a friend of the world is the enemy of God.

Epictetus, Discourses. 4.2.6
Before, when your goals consisted purely of things that are no value, your friends enjoyed your company. But you can't do well in both of two courses. No, it's inevitable that, to the degree that you're involved in one of them, you'll be a failure in the other. If you don't drink with your former drinking companions, it's impossible for them to enjoy your company to the same extent. Choose, then, whether you want to drink deep and please them or

be sober and displease them. If you don't sing with your former singing companions, it's impossible for them to love you as they did. Here too you have to choose which course you prefer.

There are many worldlings who would want to be friendly with a man who is wealthy and powerful. We should not allow our choices of association to be swayed by such externals.

John 7:24
Judge not according to the appearance, but judge righteous judgment.

James 2:2-9
For if there come unto your assembly a man with a gold ring, in goodly apparel, and there come in also a poor man in vile raiment; 3 And ye have respect to him that weareth the gay clothing, and say unto him, Sit thou here in a good place; and say to the poor, Stand thou there, or sit here under my footstool: 4 Are ye not then partial in yourselves, and are become judges of evil thoughts? 5 Hearken, my beloved brethren, Hath not God chosen the poor of this world rich in faith, and heirs of the kingdom which he hath promised to them that love him? 6 But ye have despised the poor. Do not rich men oppress you, and draw you before the judgment seats? 7 Do not they blaspheme that worthy name by the which ye are called? 8 If ye fulfil the royal law according to the scripture, Thou shalt love thy neighbour as thyself, ye do well: 9 But if ye have respect to persons, ye commit sin, and are convinced of the law as transgressors.

Seneca, Letters. 47.16

Just as one would be foolish to consider buying a horse when one hasn't inspected the animal itself but only its saddle and bridle, so it is extremely foolish to judge a human being by his clothing and his position in life. For position is only one more garment that surrounds us.

The wise man should give no heed to flattery from others who might wish to associate with him.

Mark 10:17-18

And when he was gone forth into the way, there came one running, and kneeled to him, and asked him, Good Master, what shall I do that I may inherit eternal life? 18 And Jesus said unto him, Why callest thou me good? there is none good but one, that is, God.

Seneca, Letters. 42.2

If he knew what a good man is, he would not believe himself to be one yet- indeed, he might despair of ever becoming one.

True friendship does not seek advantage from others, but it is ready and willing to make sacrifices out of love.

John 15:12-15

This is my commandment, That ye love one another, as I have loved you. 13 Greater love hath no man than this, that a man lay down his life for his friends. 14 Ye are my friends, if ye do whatsoever I command you. 15 Henceforth I call you not servants; for the servant knoweth not what his lord doeth: but I have called you friends; for all things that I have heard of my Father I have made known unto you.

Seneca, Letters. 9.10
Why make a friend? To have someone I can die for, someone I can accompany into exile, someone whose life I can save, even by laying down my own.

Seneca, Letters. 48.2
And no one can have a happy life if he looks only to himself, turning everything to his own advantage. If you want to live for yourself, you must live for another.

On Speaking

The founder of the Stoic school, Zeno of Citium, is known for the proverb, "The reason why we have two ears and only one mouth is that we might listen more and talk less." Throughout the Bible, the idea is common that wisdom is manifested in concise speech, and foolishness by unrestrained speaking.

James 1:19a
Wherefore, my beloved brethren, let every man be swift to hear, slow to speak...

James 1:26
If any man among you seem to be religious, and bridleth not his tongue, but deceiveth his own heart, this man's religion is vain.

James 3:2
For in many things we offend all. If any man offend not in word, the same is a perfect man, and able also to bridle the whole body.

Epictetus, Handbook. 33.2
Keep silence for the most part, or speak only when necessary and briefly.

Aurelius, Meditations. 3.5
Do not dress your thought in much fine talk. Be short in speech and restrained in action.

Inasmuch as speech comes from the overflow of the heart, self-restraint must begin there at the source.

Matthew 12:33-35

Either make the tree good, and his fruit good; or else make the tree corrupt, and his fruit corrupt: for the tree is known by his fruit. 34 O generation of vipers, how can ye, being evil, speak good things? for out of the abundance of the heart the mouth speaketh. 35 A good man out of the good treasure of the heart bringeth forth good things: and an evil man out of the evil treasure bringeth forth evil things.

James 3:9-12

Therewith bless we God, even the Father; and therewith curse we men, which are made after the similitude of God. 10 Out of the same mouth proceedeth blessing and cursing. My brethren, these things ought not so to be. 11 Doth a fountain send forth at the same place sweet water and bitter? 12 Can the fig tree, my brethren, bear olive berries? either a vine, figs? so can no fountain both yield salt water and fresh.

Seneca, Letters. 114.22

Let us therefore care for the mind; for from it proceed meanings and words, demeanor, facial expression, and walk. If the mind is healthy and sound, its language is likewise sturdy, strong, and virile; if the mind stumbles, the rest collapses as well.

Oaths are especially to be avoided.

Matthew 5:34-37

But I say unto you, Swear not at all; neither by heaven; for it is God's throne: 35 Nor by the earth; for it is his footstool: neither by Jerusalem; for it is the city of the great King. 36 Neither shalt thou swear by thy head, because thou canst not make one hair white or black. 37 But let your communication be, Yea, yea; Nay, nay: for whatsoever is more than these cometh of evil.

James 5:12

But above all things, my brethren, swear not, neither by heaven, neither by the earth, neither by any other oath: but let your yea be yea; and your nay, nay; lest ye fall into condemnation.

Epictetus, Handbook. 33.5

Avoid swearing oaths altogether, if that's possible, or at least as much as you can.

What to say cannot always be set in order beforehand. Sometimes the best words come only at the appropriate time.

Luke 12:11-12

And when they bring you unto the synagogues, and unto magistrates, and powers, take ye no thought how or what thing ye shall answer, or what ye shall say: 12 For the Holy Ghost shall teach you in the same hour what ye ought to say.

On Corporate Purpose

Every person in the world has a part to play, and even the lowliest of them are not without significance. Rather than seeking the most influential positions, we should be mindful of the purpose of the whole, and strive to best fulfill our purpose in whatever station we find ourselves.

1 Corinthians 12:14-18

For the body is not one member, but many. 15 If the foot shall say, Because I am not the hand, I am not of the body; is it therefore not of the body? 16 And if the ear shall say, Because I am not the eye, I am not of the body; is it therefore not of the body? 17 If the whole body were an eye, where were the hearing? If the whole were hearing, where were the smelling? 18 But now hath God set the members every one of them in the body, as it hath pleased him.

Seneca, Letters. 95.52

This universe that you see, containing the human and the divine, is a unity; we are the limbs of a mighty body. Nature brought us to birth as kin, since it generated us all from the same materials and for the same purposes, endowing us with affection for one another and making us companionable. Nature established fairness and justice. According to nature's dispensation, it is worse to harm than to be harmed. One the basis of nature's command, let our hands be available to help whenever necessary.

Epictetus, Discourses. 2.5.24-26

"What's the meaning of the saying that external things may be either in accord with nature or contrary to nature? It depends on whether or not we see ourselves as isolated entities. Consider a foot, for instance. I may think that it's normal for a foot to be clean, but if you take it as a foot, and not in isolation, it will also be appropriate for it to step in mud or on thorns, and sometimes to be amputated for the sake of the whole. Otherwise, it isn't a foot. We should think similarly of ourselves as well. What are you? A human being. If you look at yourself in isolation, it's natural for you to live to an old age, to be rich, to be healthy. But if you look at yourself as a human being and part of some whole, for the sake of that whole, it may be appropriate for you to be ill, or risk your life at sea, or be poor, or die young. Why get angry then? Don't you realize that, just as a foot taken in isolation isn't a foot, the same goes for a human being?

Epictetus, Discourses. 3.24.31-32
Don't you realize that what we're involved in is a military operation? One person has to stand guard, another go out on reconnaissance, and another even has to go out and fight. It's neither possible nor desirable for everyone to stay in the same place. But you're failing to carry out the duties assigned you by your commanding officer, you protest when you're given work that's at all demanding, and you fail to appreciate the effect you're having on the army, insofar as it's something you can effect. If everyone copied you, no one would dig a trench, erect a palisade, keep awake through the night, or expose himself to danger. Everyone would prove to be useless as a soldier.

Aurelius, Meditations. 7.13
Rational creatures are to one another as body parts are to a single organism. Reason enjoins them to cooperate in pursuit of a single aim.

On Human Equality

Slavery was common in the ancient world, and so was the idea that people are born into a certain station in life which does not change. Wisdom teaches us that each person has value as a creation of God, and therefore one is not intrinsically better than another.

Galatians 3:28
There is neither Jew nor Greek, there is neither bond nor free, there is neither male nor female: for ye are all one in Christ Jesus.

Ephesians 6:9
And, ye masters, do the same things unto them, forbearing threatening: knowing that your Master also is in heaven; neither is there respect of persons with him.

Seneca, Letters. 31.11
You must devote your efforts to that which does not deteriorate over time, and which no obstacle can bar. What is that? It is the mind- but specifically this mind, which is upright, great, and good. What else would you call it but God dwelling in a human body? This mind can be found just as well in a freedman or even a slave as in a Roman of equestrian status. For what is a Roman equestrian, or a freedman, or a slave? Those are names born of ambition or of unfair treatment. One may leap up to heaven even from a chimney corner.

Epictetus, Discourses. 1.13:3-4

Slave, won't you tolerate someone who's your own brother? He has Zeus for a father, so that he's a son born from the same seed as you and from the same heavenly sowing. Just because you've been assigned a somewhat higher station, is your immediate reaction despotism? Won't you remember what you are and who these people are over whom you have authority- that they're kinsmen, brothers by nature, offspring of Zeus?

Aurelius, Meditations. 9.22

Make haste to examine your own mind, the mind of the universe, and the mind of your neighbor. Your own mind to make sure it is just. The mind of the universe to remind yourself of what you are a part. Your neighbor's mind to figure out whether he acted knowingly or out of ignorance, and while doing this to reflect that he is your brother.

On Spending Time

The time of life is always being taken up with life's business, which often presents itself as an opportunity for gain. In reality, it is often an opportunity for loss, as time is lost in the pursuit of vanity, and there is little time left for honest reflection upon the purpose of it all. People spend the best years of their life laying in store for the worst years of life, if these are even to be reached. It is a poor trade. Life should be fully lived at the earliest opportunity.

Ephesians 5:15-17
See then that ye walk circumspectly, not as fools, but as wise, 16 Redeeming the time, because the days are evil. 17 Wherefore be ye not unwise, but understanding what the will of the Lord is.

Seneca, Letters. 1.1
Gather and guard the time that until now was being taken from you, or was stolen from you, or that slipped away. Convince yourself that what I write is true: some moments are snatched from us, some are filched, and some just vanish. But no loss is as shameful as the one that comes about through carelessness. Take a close look, and you will see that when we are not doing well, most of life slips away from us; when we are inactive, much of it- but when we are inattentive, we miss it all.

Seneca, Letters. 108.27
Let us be pleased with each new day as the best that life will give us, and so add it to our store. Life is flying away; we must catch it.

On Fearless Witness

The words of the wise are not always well received. We all have a role to play, and we must do it with courage, even if others may not understand or appreciate it.

Matthew 5:11-12
Blessed are ye, when men shall revile you, and persecute you, and shall say all manner of evil against you falsely, for my sake. 12 Rejoice, and be exceeding glad: for great is your reward in heaven: for so persecuted they the prophets which were before you.

Epictetus, Discourses. 1.29.46-49
"In what role, then, are you taking the stage now?"
"As a witness with his assignment set by God: 'Go and bear witness for me. You are my choice for playing the part of witness. Is anything not subject to will either good or bad?' 'No.' 'Do I harm anyone?' 'No.' 'Have I made what's good for each individual up to anyone other than himself?' 'No.' What testimony will you offer God? 'I'm ill fated, Lord, and miserable. No one cares for me, no one gives me anything, everyone blames me and speaks badly of me.' Is this how you're going to testify? Is that how you're going to disgrace the assignment he gave you when he conferred this honor on you and made you his choice to act as his witness in such an important manner?"

We should never be ashamed of bearing witness to truth and virtue, even if met with criticism.

Matthew 5:14-16
Ye are the light of the world. A city that is set on an hill cannot be hid. 15 Neither do men light a candle, and put it under a bushel, but on a candlestick; and it giveth light unto all that are in the house. 16 Let your light so shine before men, that they may see your good works, and glorify your Father which is in heaven.

Epictetus, Handbook. 35
When you've decided that something needs to be done and you do it, never try to conceal the fact that you're doing it, even if it's something that most people are going to have a negative opinion about. I mean, if what you are doing is wrong, avoid doing it altogether, but if it's right, why worry about misplaced criticism?

Aurelius, Mediations. 3.12
...if expecting nothing and fearing nothing, you are content to act in accord with nature and to speak with heroic honesty- then you will live well. And no power on earth can stop you.

Aurelius, Mediations. 5.3
Claim your right to say or do anything that accords with nature, and pay no attention to the chatter of your critics. If it is good to say or do something, then it is even better to be criticized for having said or done it.

Aurelius, Mediations. 5.5

Let the virtues you do possess shine forth: your honesty, dignity, and stamina; your indifference to pleasure and loathing of self-pity; your wanting little for yourself and giving much to others; your measured words and temperate deeds. Do you not recognize these as qualities you possess or as virtues you are fully capable of owning? Then why do you hide them behind a mask of false modesty and keep your bright spirit in darkness?

Conclusion

Stoicism and Christianity lived side-by-side in the early Roman Empire. They both answered the important questions as to the meaning and purpose of life. While they sometimes offered similar answers, however; their differences were fundamental to the core.

The Stoic fixation upon death goes beyond a mere mental exercise for putting life in perspective. For the Stoic, suicide is always an option if circumstances were to become unbearable. To die is to be reabsorbed into the universe, and can be taken as an exit from this life as needed. For the Christian, suicide is dishonorable– a cowardly and sinful murder of self, which shows a lack of faith in divine providence.

The Stoic idea of universal order extends to the State, and for an individual to sacrifice himself for the good of the State is honorable. For the Christian, the individual has intrinsic value, and the State is to be regarded only inasmuch as it acts in accordance with its divine purpose to uphold justice and restrain evil. If the State promotes injustice, civil disobedience is appropriate, as one must obey God rather than men. For the Stoic, oblations to the gods are the patriotic duty of a good citizen. For the Christian, they are blasphemous acts of worship to demons, and can never be practiced under any circumstance.

The Stoic outlook on the afterlife is cautiously optimistic. Life will continue according to the rational principle of the universe, but your personal existence is immaterial to this. The Christian hope is for a personal conscious eternity in the presence of God and all the saints.

The main point of departure is on the resurrection of the dead. While the Stoics imagine a glorious future when all life returns to God who gave it, it is impersonal and intangible. While life might be reconstituted in other forms, it makes no sense to them to hope for a new body which would be recognizable in the same pattern as the current one. Without the resurrection of the dead; however, there is no real underlying purpose for self-denial in this life. Without a resurrection, what would be the point of enduring pain or death courageously? Would not one rather live only for the enjoyment of this life, as the Epicureans do?

> 1 Corinthians 15:32
> If after the manner of men I have fought with beasts at Ephesus, what advantageth it me, if the dead rise not? let us eat and drink; for to morrow we die.

Not only does Christianity offer hope for a more tangible afterlife, it also gives hope for better opportunities in this life. The Stoic conception of God is more mechanistic– you are just one infinitesimally small piece of a grand and intricate arrangement of the universe, and fate assigns to you a specific function. Christianity tells of how God loves you personally, you can pray to him for various outcomes. This does not mean that God will always give you what you want, but that you can actively participate in the outworking of his plan for your life through your choices.

The Stoics regarded the ultimate test as facing death with resolute fortitude; but when they saw the Christian martyrs, they did not appreciate their courage, but it appeared to them as sheer obstinance.

Epictetus, Discourses. 4.7.4,6

Imagine someone, then, who's completely indifferent about whether he lives or dies, and willingly accepts his lot: when he comes into a tyrant's presence, what's to stop him from doing so without fear?

...So madness can make a person regard these things with indifference, and so can habit: witness the Galileans.

Aurelius, Meditations. 11.3

How lovely the soul that is prepared- when its hour comes to slough off this flesh- for extinction, dispersion, or survival! But this readiness should result from a personal decision, not from sheer contrariness like the Christians, and manifest itself deliberately and soberly, in a convincing manner, without histrionics.

Somehow the public deaths of the Christians made an impression on the minds of many, however; and over time with their changed lives and new teaching the Christians would sway the Roman Empire up to the point where Constantine could declare it the new imperial religion.

So many centuries later, as Christianity has long been the dominant worldview in Western Civilization, it is now giving way to various other ways of thinking and living. Stoicism seems to be a long-forgotten alternative, which has been resurrected to challenge us again. Let us embrace the contest, and be made better for it.

Made in United States
North Haven, CT
27 December 2024

63640438R00061